THE

DAILY

GRIND

HOW TO OPEN & RUN A COFFEE SHOP

THAT MAKES MONEY

THE

DAILY

GRIND

HOW TO OPEN & RUN A COFFEE SHOP

THAT MAKES MONEY

Andrew & Claire Bowen

2015

Andrew & Claire Bowen

First Printing: 2015

ISBN-13: 978-1519365705
ISBN-10:1519365705

www.dailygrindbook.com

www.cafesuccesshub.com

Dedication

For Sarah & Gregory

Thank you for your support and encouragement

along our journey.

Table of Contents

<u>Acknowledgements</u>

We would like to thank the following people for all their help and support during the writing of this book.

Damian Mark Smyth

John Richardson (The Coffee Boys)

Sheena Gilson

Peter Austen

Martyn Herriott (The Beverage Standards Association)

Peter Gilson

Martin Logan

Dylis Guyan

Costas Kkolos

Gary Spinks

Foreword

I'm often asked which books, other than our own, potential coffee shop owners should read and my usual answer is 'all of them'. The point really is that it's such a tough business, with such a high failure rate, that you really need to be armed with as much knowledge as possible.

The slightly harsh fact is that some of the books on running coffee shops, whilst nearly always having some decent nuggets of information, are a little frustrating. In many cases they're based on the musings of a journalist who has never opened or run a coffee shop or on the experiences of someone who has owned one coffee shop and feels that what they've learnt is gospel and can apply across the board. In a few cases this has resulted in what I regard as fundamentally flawed advice.

This is not the case with this book. I've known Andrew and Claire for many years now and have the utmost respect for them. When we met they were going through some difficult issues with a franchisor and the awareness of these kinds of problems is exactly what is necessary to write a useful book.

They are hugely experienced in the industry and, more importantly, over several locations. This has resulted in a highly practical book with some very sound advice. They have a very interesting take on some of the issues that Hugh Gilmartin (my fellow Coffee Boy) and I talk about. The suggestion to regard your 'rent and rates as part of your marketing spend' is a brilliant way to express a tricky issue and I'll certainly be quoting that again.

Their advice on the value of reliability and consistency to the customer is something that cannot be emphasised enough. Far too often we see new starts obsessing over details that don't matter to the customer and forgetting what they really want.

It's also great to see the 'man in the brown suit' story rolled out again. This moment was arguably the most important lesson of my business career and the message cannot be stressed too many times – know your numbers!

One final piece of advice that they offer is something that our research shows is almost always ignored – work out the price you want for your business... before you open the doors. There's great wisdom in that and if genuinely worked through can avoid a lot of pain in the future.

So make sure you read it with a marker pen in your hand. And most importantly of all take their advice – it might just prevent you from making some very expensive mistakes.

John Richardson

www.thecoffeeboys.com

<u>Preface</u>

In all the excitement of opening your first coffee shop, everything is new; the scale can be large with the bright lights of success waiting for you to grasp your big moment.

But where do you turn for advice that you can trust, to make near as damn it certain that you will deliver your dream?

If you choose a franchise, tread carefully; the franchisor wants their share of money from your hard work and efforts. A less risky option? - It often isn't.

The bank manager is happy as long as they have your house as collateral, then their risk is minimal.

The sad reality is that there's nowhere to learn how to run a coffee shop; no university course, no NVQ, no advice readily available to the fledgling entrepreneur looking to make their mark..... until now that is!

Over twenty years experience of coffee shop ownership between us; what worked, what didn't and all the bits that gel the business together, like a good bean to the perfect cuppa, have been brought together for the first time in 'The Daily Grind', a book for current and budding coffee shop owners.

So many people have asked us for our advice, that we felt it our duty to share our experience, so 'The Daily Grind' was conceived. A book where you can get honest, unbiased advice and information from two people who have actually; been franchisees, developed their own small independent chain of coffee shops, dealt with crisis and success, taken over existing businesses and opened from scratch.

This book is just about the coffee shop business. We talk about the nitty-gritty detail, which most business books don't cover, including real life examples of what has worked and not worked for us on our journey. Because we still run our business we are right up to date with what it feels like to be a coffee shop owner in today's market.

We both gave up our well-paid jobs ten years ago to open our first coffee shop. We started as franchisees taking over an existing coffee shop, doubled the sales in two months and within three months had our second coffee shop. Because of our success we became regional franchisees within six months and had opened our third branch twelve months later.

We moved on to develop our own small chain of independent coffee shops turning over a million pounds a year, so have first-hand experience in every aspect of running the business; from dealing with lawyers, suppliers, local authorities, landlords, builders, architects and designers, to recruiting a great team, delivering exceptional customer service and marketing.

The buzz we got from opening our coffee shops and moulding them to become local institutions is amazing.

When we started out there were only two routes to opening a coffee shop; either take a franchise and take on their brand and systems at a great cost or start up on your own with little support and work it out as you went along, again at great cost.

Our passion and drive, combined with the ability to build relationships with our team, our guests and our suppliers, has been instrumental in our success.

With the insights and details from this book and the supporting website www.dailygrindbook.com it is now possible to have the systems of a franchise, with the individuality of an independent.

We have found a way to be as efficient as the big chains and make a connection with our guests that our big rivals would only ever aspire to achieve.

Introduction

This book is set out in a logical progression, mirroring the stages a budding entrepreneur takes in the journey of opening a new coffee shop. It can be read as separate chapters or all together.

The principles and ideas are from our experience of owning and running coffee shops and we share what worked and what didn't work for us.

There was so much information and detail that we wanted to add, so it is supported by our two websites; www.dailygrindbook.com will provide direct references from this book, www.cafesuccesshub.com is filled with information, ideas and resources that will help you on your journey to becoming a coffee shop entrepreneur.

This book contains expert tips and guidance on the things you really need to know:

- Choosing the look and feel of your shop
- Developing your core values that your customers buy into
- Finding a site that attracts cash like a magnet to your business
- Attracting and recruiting the right team

- Making a success out of your investment

- Becoming the social hub of your community

- Explaining all the legal aspects that you need to be aware of

- Keeping the crowd returning to buy more from you

- Effortlessly matching your operation to the size of your market

We hope that this book will challenge your thinking and prepare you for opening and running your coffee shop that makes money.

Please join in the conversation on Facebook.

www.facebook.com/dailygrindbook/

Don't Open Your Coffee Shop Until You Have Read This....

With apologies to Benjamin Franklin, 'in this world nothing can be certain but death, taxes and that everyone knows how to run a coffee shop.'

A coffee shop is one of the easiest and cheapest types of hospitality business to open. This low barrier to entry is attractive and a main reason why people choose to open a coffee shop over a restaurant or a pub.

What people fail to realise is that unlike a restaurant or a pub, the average transaction value for a coffee shop is much lower, so it must attract many more guests than a the restaurant or pub with the same overheads to break even.

When people come to us for advice, it can be for a variety of different reasons, but the questions we ask them are always the same. The answers to these questions will provide clarity of the understanding they will need before they proceed further down the road to their first coffee shop.

Why?

You need to clarify your WHY so that everyone knows what you stand for. It's so much easier then, to plan a range, select a location, recruit a team and attract guests, if this is crystal clear in your mind. You must be able to articulate it in one sentence. Your WHY will build trust in your team and guests alike, as they will understand what you stand for as a business. Your WHY is a belief that incorporates your core values.

There is so much competition in the coffee shop market, it's impossible to compete on price alone. A low price strategy never leads to the loyalty of your guests, as they will always buy from the cheapest.

Important questions we ask when deciding your WHY are:

- Why are you considering opening a coffee shop?
- What's going to make your coffee shop better than the competition?
- Why will people visit you?

These are questions that many people don't even think about. It's probably one of the most important things to get right in your head before you start. Without answering these questions, everything you do going forward will be compromised. For example, your WHY could be; to share your passion for coffee and educate your guests that there is life after Starbucks, or to sell your handmade cakes, with your special recipe that you know everyone will love, and make guests flock to your door.

When you have refined your WHY, it makes it so much easier to answer the rest of the questions that need answering before you can open. This will drive your selection of the location, design, marketing, recruitment and pretty much everything else.

Who?

Important questions we always ask are; who are you, what is your experience, and what are your expectations of your business?

There is a widely held belief that anybody can run a coffee shop and make money. It's often a lot of people's dream to open a little coffee shop on the high street or in a quaint village. The fact of the matter is that in the early days it's hard work, it is long hours and it can be very challenging. The successful coffee shop owner needs to be very resilient and resourceful.

Who are you going to get to help you?

Why would you spend a penny without taking professional advice, from experienced and trusted people? Many people regret for years to come not taking the advice of people who have done it before, who understand the risks and know how to reduce them.

You will need a great accountant and a great property lawyer to make sure that you set up your business and leases correctly. You should also consider taking the advice of people who have a great depth of experience in the coffee shop business. Taking good advice from books, such as this, will ultimately save you thousands of pounds and your sanity.

How?

How are you going to raise the money and ensure you have enough working capital?

How are you going to secure a lease on a property? How are you going to decide what coffee to sell and what range to offer? How are you going to recruit and how are you going to market your new business?

You will need to find great advice with the legal aspects and to build relationships with banks or your backers.

What?

What type of business do you want to run? Do you want to work in it every day, or employ others to run it? Do you want to expand and have ten shops in ten years?

Most people will say that they would like to open a chain of coffee shops, however unless the first coffee shop is a massive financial success and all the routines and processes are buttoned down, this will be highly unlikely.

Where?

Your location will be easier to pinpoint when you know the style of coffee shop you want to open. The next chapter, The Clever Coffee Shop Location, will help you choose a great place to open.

Summary

Once you have answered these questions you can then define your ideal guest or avatar that will love your business. Then when you open, everything about your business will attract your ideal guests.

The number one reason people visit a coffee shop is always its location, so getting this right is paramount for your success.

Spending time understanding yourself and your vision for your coffee shop before starting is essential for success.

A great book, to get your head around what happens in the life cycle of an entrepreneurial business, is 'The E Myth Revisited', by Michael Gerber (Gerber). This is recommended reading for all prospective coffee shop owners. It takes you through the essential stages of opening and running a business for the first time.

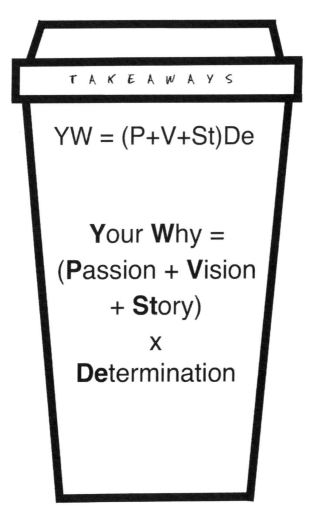

TAKEAWAYS

YW = (P+V+St)De

Your **W**hy =
(**P**assion + **V**ision
+ **St**ory)
x
Determination

The Clever Coffee Shop Location

We have put this section together following our experience opening sites and have captured the key issues you need to consider when selecting a site for your coffee shop.

A convenient location is the number one reason that people say they visit a coffee shop. Getting this right is fundamental in the success of your business. The second and third reasons are consistency and service, which we cover later in this book.

We have not specifically mentioned high street versus shopping centre, as the criteria works for both.

Use the checklist downloadable from the following site to score the cleverness of the location and building:

www.dailygrindbook.com/resources

Local competition

Busy local cafés are sometimes a good thing

It's not always a bad thing to have lots of other cafés close to you, as often the area becomes a destination for people when they are hungry or thirsty. Most people will want a variety of establishments to choose from on different days, so being around other eating establishments is not always a bad thing.

No chains is sometimes a bad thing

Although you may think that not having the big players close by is a good thing, the chances are that if you think it's a great area to open, then so will they. There is also a strong possibility that they would open close by in the future thus reducing your trade and therefore the viability of your site. If they are already open, you need to consider the following. Is there enough trade for you both? Will you be different enough from them to attract a big enough guest base? What weaknesses do they have in their site and how can you use them to help you?

Are you a me-too or unique?

If your coffee shop is going to be similar to what is already available in that location, i.e. a me-too, then you will need to find a way to give your guests a compelling reason to visit you. Either by being the best or by having some unique stand out features. The more similar you are to your competition, the less competitive you will be. The ideal situation is that your coffee shop will complement what is already available locally, rather than directly compete.

Is it a brand or an independent street/location?

Areas tend to build their own identity over time, so work out whether your chosen location is mainly independents or branded businesses or a mixture of both. If it's mainly independents and a good mix, then you will probably be ok. If it's all large corporate businesses, then your offer may not work, as the guest mind-set will be to play safe and go corporate.

Footfall

Knowing the times of high passing trade

Spend a lot of time understanding when the peaks and troughs of the footfall are. Visit the area on different days and at different times, to do a footfall count. Consider only one in a hundred people becoming guests and put it into your business model.

How many days a week will it be cost effective for you to open?

Is the area quiet at weekends, such as a business park or college area? You will need to know your daily breakeven target, which we cover in the Financial Controls chapter later. If the cost of the team and utilities will not be covered by the daily sales, then that will tell you if you can't afford to open on those quiet days.

Reason for guest journey, i.e. do potential guests have the time or reason to come in?

Just because people are walking past your door, it doesn't mean that they are potential guests of yours. We have seen businesses that are located between two stations that have massive passing trade but because everyone is on a mission to catch a connection, they are not in the right mind-set to go in.

If there is a big office block close by with thousands of people in and out, that might be good but if there is a subsidized café in the building, then you will not attract many of those people.

How many guests can you serve per hour?

When the footfall is high overall but is condensed over a limited time e.g. the morning rush, then factor in the maximum guests you can serve per hour. If there are a thousand people walking past your location between 8:30 and 9:00 am, you would only be able to physically serve about sixty of these people and your queue would be long and off putting to others.

Size and shape

Size is important

If your location is too small, you will need lots of take away trade to compensate. If it is too big, you may never look full and the rent and fit out will cost more. We recommend a minimum of fifty covers.

The shape of the space is important too, a long thin unit or a wide unit without much depth will be harder to get right when you are trying to create the right ambience.

That's not to say you need an empty square box, as having features to incorporate in the design will be good but you need to consider queuing space and guest flow through the building.

Room for toilet/disabled toilet/baby change?

Factor in the size and location of the toilet. Although in some instances you are not legally required to provide toilets, not having a toilet will be detrimental on your trade. If your potential guests include young families, then baby changing is essential and likewise if your avatar is elderly, then a disabled toilet facility is a must.

Will the site accommodate the equipment needed?

Try and visualize the position of counters, equipment and storage. Will there be enough room left for your guests? How many covers will you comfortably be able to arrange and what type of seating are you planning to use?

Outside seating area

This is a great opportunity that really helps you trade all year round. It generates a proper café style environment and attracts guests. If you provide a canopy, then it becomes an all year round seating area. If you can add outside heating, then that will be a bonus. Consider if the area would be an attractive place to sit and watch the world go by, with lots going on or is it annoyingly noisy or windy.

Smoking area

Guests will want to smoke outside whether you like it or not, but you will need to prevent smoke from coming back inside the premises. Consider if this will be possible.

In sunshine- morning or afternoon or both?

The sunny side will always be an advantage, so if you are in competition with other seating areas, the seats in the sun will always fill up first! Consider the prevailing wind as well as that will make a difference to the guest's enjoyment.

Number of outside seats

If you can maximize the number of covers by using outside seating, are you able to store them somewhere at night?

Any restrictions to outside seating?

You would need to find out if you need to pay extra to have seats outside, i.e. if you don't own or rent the frontage, then the local authority will almost certainly charge you and add restrictions as to where and when you can put the chairs out and how many tables and chairs you can use. Don't assume the local authority will grant you permission.

Orientation

On the sunny side of the street?

In the same way that outside seating in the sun has an advantage, then a location on the sunny side of the street has the advantage too, attracting more passing trade. Consider the direction of the prevailing wind too, as that will also determine the route people take when walking on that street.

A corner site is an advantage

Corner sites always make good coffee shops. You benefit from the great footfall of both roads and the double frontage of the building has more glass. Check the rateable value of the site, as they are generally more expensive. The rates are based on the size of a building, as well as how much of the space is near the front of the building.

On the same side as the bus stops and shops?

If you are on the same side as the bus stops and shops, then that is an advantage as well, as people will pass closer.

No barriers to entry? e.g. a busy road

The less physical barriers to your business the better; busy roads, underpasses, pelican crossings, pedestrian barriers etc. will all deter people from visiting you.

On the side of the street that people walk?

Check the side of the road that people typically walk on and if you are not on that side then again you will be disadvantaged.

Building style

Good frontage with big windows is an advantage

As with restaurants, people are more likely to come in if they can see similar people enjoying a good atmosphere through the window. So having the ability to see inside is very important. The size of the windows may be limited by the style of the building but they should always offer a good view inside.

Will it be congruent with your style of offer?

Consider if you can adapt your design elements to fit the existing building, so that it comes in line with your offer. If a building looks like an old tearoom how could you make it fit as a trendy café? The look of the building will be a key element in attracting your future guests, so it needs to be working as a marketing tool for you all day long.

Level entry with a wide enough door for wheelchairs and buggies

Getting a level entrance, without steps, is important in attracting young families with buggies and the elderly or disabled. Having a wide enough easy to open door, will be an advantage for those with special access needs. A level entrance door is always a big advantage, as carrying hot drinks up and down steps will be a cause of concern for people.

How will your signage fit in?

Having great signage will be an important part of your on going marketing, so have a look at similar local businesses to see the style of their signs. If you can see that they have a similar style to the one you have planned, then there is no problem. However if your proposed signage is much bigger, or illuminated, where the existing one is not, then you will need to check with the planning department of your local council to see what will be permitted. If you open until late then an illuminated sign is important. Also, if you are on an estate or shopping mall, you might be able to acquire rights to have your signage on the main estate signs that show the tenants on the estate.

Age of building for maintenance issues and running costs e.g. heating

When you sign the commercial lease you will always be liable for the maintenance of the area you lease, so beware of the age of a building and the potential threats. The running costs will make a big impact to your break-even.

Access to the building for deliveries and efficiency

Check whether you have to service the unit from the front, or if there is potential to service from the rear. If there is a designated service area, ensure you obtain a right to use that area in your lease.

Building readiness

Power - big enough distribution board and 3-phase

Check the distribution board as you will need enough circuits for the coffee machine, oven, grill, dishwasher, hand dryers and air-conditioning /ventilation. Some larger coffee machines and ovens use 3-phase power so you need to make sure that you have sufficient supply. This can be very expensive to sort out, as you may need a new consumer board, costing a few thousand pounds or even more and the power supplied to the premises by the electricity board may be potentially tens of thousands pounds.

The fundamental infrastructure works to the unit (e.g. upgrading the electricity supply) will often be something that the landlord is prepared to carry out himself, to allow you to fit out the property. The landlord is likely to want you to be contractually committed to taking the unit before he will undertake these works.

Ventilation and air-conditioning

Every coffee shop needs good ventilation and cooling; all the equipment produces heat, so heating is less of an issue than cooling. You will need to be able to maintain a good ambient temperature in the building, otherwise people will complain and misted up windows are not attractive. Air con units are often to be located outside of your unit, on another part of the landlord's property. Make sure the landlord would give you the right to place it there and the right to access it, to maintain and repair the units.

Extraction

Depending on the style of food you are considering, you may need to have extract ducts, but these often need planning permission. The coffee shop should smell of coffee and not of fried foods, so extraction will be important depending on your menu.

Storage

Think about where you will be able to store your dry goods and place your fridges and freezers. Will they be accessible and easy to get to when you are busy. Ensure you have enough storage area.

Shape

Rectangular is best; wide enough for the counter, some tables and passing space at the entrance. You should consider the different types of areas you will need for the guests to do different things. For example, you'll need a place for groups to use for working or meetings and somewhere for people on their own to sit and watch the world go by. You may want a combination of tall chairs and low chairs, as well as soft and hard seating. Consider the possibility of room dividers to improve privacy and intimacy.

Floors

Ground floor units are the best. Those that are first floor will need extra marketing to compensate. Remember, a first floor will be 75% less attractive to guests, as nobody likes climbing stairs. They might not even know the upstairs exists.

Room for bins

Will you have room for two wheelie bins; a recycle and a general waste bin? You may need more than two bins depending on the recycling services in your area. Where are you able to put your wheelie bins or waste for collection? You may find that the landlord has a communal area for bins and if so, you should ensure you get a right to use that area in your lease. Otherwise you may need to place your bins in your unit.

Able to be cleaned easily?

Cleaning will be one of your biggest daily tasks, so having a building that is easy to clean will save you a lot of time and money over the life of your coffee shop. Are the windows easy to clean and are there any difficult areas that you will need to get contractors in to clean?

Utilities- where do they come into the building?

Find out where the water, electricity and gas come into the building from the road or outside. Will there be any problem getting those services to the areas that you need them inside? Any major change of this will be expensive.

Drainage - in relation to counters sinks and toilets -wherever possible do not use pumps

Check where the drains are, in comparison to your counters and toilets. Avoid using pumps wherever possible as typically these will only break when you are most busy or away on holiday, causing you the most problems. Plan to use four-inch drainpipes wherever possible from the sinks, because coffee grinds and milk fat will block your drains. You will also need a good fall on the pipes to insure they don't get blocked.

Ergonomics for productivity

Having things in the right place will speed up the production process. Anything you do to reduce the productivity of your team, such as fridges being a long way from the counters, will become a fixed cost in your business, as it will make it more difficult for your team to do their job, and reduce the number of guests you will be able to serve.

Cost of fitting out the unit

Check out what is in a good condition and will be able to be used in your coffee shop. New floors and ceilings are expensive and will slow down the fit out time. Ventilation will often need planning permission to vent to the outside of the building. The more you can adapt, the cheaper it will be. Ensure suitable or adaptable lighting and factor in running costs.

Insurance - are there any extra costs?

Consider insurance costs, for example, a thatched roof, listed buildings and particularly flooding risks. Check with local people if they know of any time when the area was flooded. Do you need a burglar alarm or CCTV as a stipulation of insurance? You will need to arrange your own contents and shop frontage insurance, whereas the landlord will usually arrange the buildings insurance and pass on the cost to you. Factor this into your costing. You need to ensure you shop around for a good quote and remember the landlord won't necessarily do this.

Landlords consent

You will need the landlord's approval of your proposed fit out by way of an additional legal document called a 'license for alterations'. The licence should ensure that your fit out improvements to the property are not taken in to account at a rent review, otherwise you will be paying a higher rent following a rent review!

The licence for alterations should set out whether or not you will need to remove your fit out at the end of the lease. Quite often landlords will require the property to be returned to them in the condition they provided it.

WIFI

Make sure you are permitted to have a Wi-Fi service, as clients expect that now. Believe it or not, there may be a restriction on this so always check.

Andrew & Claire Bowen

Car parking

Local car parks

The cost of car parking and the method of payment will both affect the length and frequency of visits. The difference between pay on exit and pay and display, is that the former will allow your guests to stay a little longer and spend a little more without worrying about going over the time on the pay and display ticket.

On street

If you have on street parking nearby, that is a bonus. As well as helping your trade, it will help you park outside your own business without worrying when you need to leave.

Complementary businesses or services nearby

If you have lots of businesses close by that have a waiting time for the service to be completed, then that will be a great benefit. You could even do joint ventures with these businesses to encourage their guests to come to you while they wait, before or after the event.

He is a list of good types of businesses that would be great to have close by:

- Theatre
- Bus station

- Garage
- Cinema
- Anywhere where there is a waiting time for the service to be completed - e.g. tyre fitters
- Taxi ranks
- Markets
- Train station
- Parks

Local authority restrictions

A3 planning?

Lots of coffee shops used to be able to run on A1 (general shop) planning permission, but many authorities now need them to have A3 (restaurant) planning permission. The difference is, there is a limit to the number of A3 licences allowed in certain areas, so depending on the local authority planning guidelines, you may have a problem if you don't check it out before you start any work. You will need to check with the local authority what planning needs to be in place as some require A1, some require A3 and some require mixed A1/A3. If planning is not in place, work out who will obtain the planning and whether this will need to be done before or after you are contractually committed to taking the lease. Check the conditions in the planning consent, as these may impact on your trade, such as restrictions on trading hours.

Beware the unscrupulous landlord that will wait for you to get improved planning permission for their site and then increase the rent or worse still not sign a lease.

Fire escapes

Ensure there are sufficient fire escapes for the unit, as a lack of fire escapes may result in fewer covers being permitted in the unit, hitting your revenue. For high street units, in particular check the access of rear fire escapes.

Licences

If you plan to sell alcohol you will need to look into any potential restrictions. You should take professional advice on this.

Extraction

If you're planning to have a coffee roaster, then you will need extraction, which in turn will need permission from the local authority if not already present.

Opening times

Look around at other local businesses; see what time they are open from and to. Find out if there are any restrictions particularly in a shopping centre? If you open later you will miss one of your busiest periods of trade in the morning

Litter

Sometimes local businesses are made to collect litter from an area, not just outside their building. So check this out.

Outside seats

If there is space for roadside seats, find out how much it will cost per table or chair, or per square meter. Work out what additional cost this will be for your business and if it is profitable.

Listed building status

This is a question worth asking. Sometimes a feature of your building may be protected even if the whole building is not and any change to that would not be allowed.

Any signage restrictions?

Check if you are allowed A boards on the pavement or projecting signs. As mentioned before, new illuminated signs may need planning permission. You will want to get the biggest and most visible signage you are allowed to put up. This will act as 24/7 marketing for you and is a really important point.

Rent, rates and leases

When dealing with property law you need to take professional advice before agreeing or signing anything. Property law is filled with traps and it's all written in confusing language. Signing a bad lease could be the most expensive thing you ever do. Think about the lease as a commitment to spend the annual lease times the number of years you sign up for.

Max 10% of net sales for both rent and rates

As a general rule of thumb your rent and rates combined should be no more than 10% of your projected net sales.

Consider your rents and rates as parts of your marketing spend!

If you need to spend more on a great site, consider the extra spend which will get you a better location and more guests, as a marketing cost. If you could take a cheaper site and spend less than this difference in marketing to fill up your shop, then it's worth getting the cheapest site.

Potential for a rent free period

Depending on the area and market, it is often possible to get a rent-free period from your landlord, so it's always worth asking the question. Between three and six months is the norm.

Extra costs

Take into account the costs of stamp duty, land tax and the costs of registering your lease at the land registry.

Break clauses in your lease

A vital part of any lease agreement for you, is the break clause, i.e. when you are able to leave the lease without having to pay anything. Landlords don't like these, they are generally built in when there is a rent review and often there are timescales you must follow to allow you to exercise this right and sometimes timescales are difficult on purpose. It is advisable to get a one year break clause built-in because at the end of twelve months you will know if your business is profitable or not.

Personal guarantees

It is often required that you provide a personal guarantee on the lease. Try and avoid this at all costs, it is more preferable to offer a rent deposit.

Lease length

The landlord will always want you to sign up for the longest lease possible; this is because it increases the value of his property if he wants to sell it. Conversely, you will need a lease of sufficient length to ensure that you are able to recoup your investment and have security that your business will not be closed because the lease is up.

The Landlord and Tenant Act (1954)

Whether or not your lease is within The Landlord and Tenant Act will depend on your negotiating strength. As a small independent operator, you would do well to get the lease within the act. The benefit of being inside the act is that it affords you extra protections and the landlord cannot simply evict you at the end of the tenancy.

When are the rent reviews?

When you agree the rent, you also agree a rent review date. This is when the landlord will try and put up your rent. Therefore the less rent review dates you have the better.

Any additional costs e.g. service contracts

Rent and rates are not the only costs you are sometimes liable for. If you are in a shared building, then you will be liable for some of the costs of running that building. These are called service charges and sometimes they can be as much as the rates, so beware.

Will the landlord help with the cost of fit out?

Sometimes the landlord will help you with the cost of fitting out or adapting the building for your use. Again this is worth asking for, as generally this increases the value of the property for the landlord as well.

Shared liabilities for building repair?

As well as service contracts you should watch out for any shared liabilities. For example, you may be on the ground floor of the building but be liable for a proportion of the repair of the roof.

Recent uses & local successes and failures

What was the unit used for before

If a shop is empty, you need to find out why it is empty. What was it was used for before and why did it close?

How many cafés have opened and closed quickly nearby?

Investigate how many successful new cafés have opened or closed nearby, as sometimes a unit or an area is a graveyard of businesses.

Speak to local businesses

As you would do if you were buying a house, have a beer in the local pub and speak to local businesses about what they think of the area; whether it is up and coming or losing guests. Find out if there is any new big development being planned that will change the centre of gravity of the town centre and make the area that you are considering opening in, look and feel completely different.

Resale value

Has the unit a viable other use?

At some stage it is likely that you will want to sell your business or close it down. So the more viable uses your unit has, the better.

What is the re-assignment of lease restrictions?

Sometimes a landlord is happy for you to sublet the building. This might be an option in the future if it was available to you.

Check the dilapidation criteria

Like any tenant when you come to leave the property, you will be liable to bring the shop back to its former state. Sometimes the dilapidation clause is very expensive to fulfil, so it's worth checking carefully before you sign the lease.

Have an exit strategy

When drafting your lease consider how easy it will be to assign the lease or the possibility of subletting the unit to another tenant and you becoming their landlord. Ultimately you might be able to surrender your lease back to the landlord, but remember that when you sign a lease you are signing up to pay the full amount of rent for the whole period of the lease, which the landlord is legally entitled to claim.

Landlord

Do you pay monthly or quarterly in advance?

During the recession many businesses have paid their rent monthly in advance, rather than quarterly. This is good for your cash flow so you should ask for it.

Is there a rent premium?

If you're looking at an occupied unit, and if it's in a very popular area, you may need to pay a rent premium to the current tenant, where there is a lease assignment and they are prepared to give up the lease to you.

Will you be able to build a relationship with the landlord to enable changes?

Having a good relationship with your landlord will be very important, and timely two-way communication will be vital in maintaining this relationship. The odd call, your email to him or her about their property and what's going on locally, will be helpful for both of you.

Are they a corporate or individual landlord?

It's often more difficult to deal with corporate landlords rather than individuals. The people you do the deal with in a corporate business, will often not have full autonomy and can be moved on quickly, so you may be dealing with different people during your tenancy.

Does he own the freehold?

It's not uncommon for the landlord to not own the freehold of the building and there will possibly be other restrictions that you need to find out about that will be in that contract.

Franchising

This subject is another whole book but in terms of this chapter; from a property perspective there are a couple of differing leasehold structures that can be set up and you would need to take legal advice on them. It is however, as a general principle, going to be the franchisor that tells you as franchisee what you can and cannot do and you will be obliged to follow.

Sometimes the franchisor will take the head lease and then sublet to you. Other times they will expect you to take the head lease but include in their franchise agreement with you, how you can utilize the unit.

Summary

The number one reason people visit a coffee shop is its location. The biggest fixed overhead for your business is likely to be the rent and rates. A great location will also be worth more money when it comes time to sell.

Getting these elements right are at the heart of your success but failing to spend sufficient time getting them right will be a very expensive error.

The checklist that supports this chapter is available to download from www.dailygrindbook.com/resources

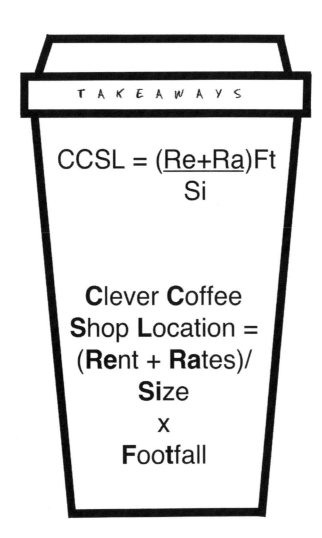

TAKEAWAYS

$$CCSL = \frac{(Re+Ra)Ft}{Si}$$

Clever **C**offee **S**hop Location = (**Re**nt + **Ra**tes)/ **Si**ze x Footfall

The Team

The manager- the most important piece of the puzzle

It's very tempting when you open your first coffee shop to try and do everything yourself, because it's your idea, your baby and your passion. It is quite possible to do everything yourself and very rewarding in the first few months, but it soon gets very tiring and you lose passion. You will find it tedious and time-consuming to do all the day-to-day running of the business, as well as being an entrepreneur and an innovator.

In his book 'The E-Myth Revisited', Michael Gerber (Gerber) describes how the entrepreneur becomes a technician in their business very quickly; that is they move from the ideas and creative role into a doer that's sapping all their energy and makes them wonder why they ever started in the first place.

If you decide not to get a manager and do it all yourself to begin with, you should at least look at recruiting people who have the potential for a management role to support you. You should quickly allocate responsibilities for tasks and start documenting all processes and routines that you have developed, so that they can be taught to the rest of the team and be useful new starter inductions.

Pay as much to the team as you can afford and reward well

Attracting and retaining a great team will be a key element in the success of your coffee shop. We recommend that you pay above the local going rate to attract the best candidates in your area. A well-trained and motivated team will be a vital point of difference between your business and your competitors. Your team are likely to stay with you for longer as well.

One of the hidden costs that few people consider is the cost of labour turnover. That is how much it costs in lost productivity, disappointed guests, wages and margin when you train a new person from scratch.

A number of things happen when somebody leaves and somebody starts. The old team becomes a new team because of the new addition; they then start again to go through the stages of team building from the start. Donald B Egolf (Egolf) 'Forming Storming Norming Performing: Successful Communication in Groups And Teams', describes perfectly what your team goes through.

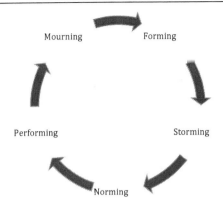

Forming: When a team is new, there is uncertainty of job roles, lots of input is needed from the manager and the team starts to test the boundaries.

Storming: This is the stage where team members vie for position within the team and often ends in arguments and misunderstandings.

Norming: Things settle down, people know how they fit into the team and learn their role better.

Performing: At this stage the team gels and the manager needs very little input to steer the ship.

Mourning: When a team member leaves and another joins, the process starts over again.

All this impacts on the efficiency and effectiveness of the team. The effect on productivity of a new team member on the team is shown on the following graph. When someone joins a team they actually have an overall negative effect on the team productivity and although they are an extra pair of hands, the amount of guidance and training they need, will impact on the other team members.

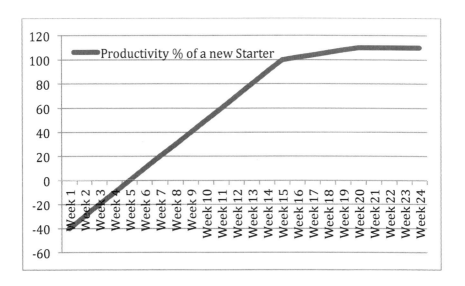

A new starter will therefore reduce the overall productivity of the team during the early stages of their training and perhaps take six to eight weeks to become a hundred percent efficient. They can then take up to six months to achieve the same level of productivity as the rest of the team who typically over perform and add more value.

There are less obvious costs of taking on a new starter, like not knowing the guests and their regular drinks, or making mistakes which affect margin and waste.

So once you know this, you can calculate the cost to your business of labour turnover. If you then invest in your existing team in terms of higher wages and better training, that will be a much better use of your money.

A business owner once told me that he was worried about training his team too well because they might leave but I told him the alternative would be not train them and they might stay.

The emotional cycle of change

A universal principle well worth knowing about is the emotional cycle of change. Simply put, every time a person experiences a change of any type they will go through the same feelings:

1. Uniformed optimism – when they hear about a change and are positive about it but don't know what to expect.
2. Informed pessimism – they have thought about what effect the change will have on them and are worried.
3. Depths of despair – the change has started and they don't like it.
4. Informed optimism – the change was not as bad as they thought and they are getting used to it.
5. Acceptance – the change has happened and they are happy and working at full performance.

You and your team will experience this every day, sometimes every hour. It is the skill of the manager to take people through these stages, as quickly as possible and to understand that when you are dealing with how people feel, empathy is required.

Ground rules

A really useful exercise for you to do with your team, is to agree a set of ground rules about the behaviour you all expect of each other. Print these off and put them in a prominent position in the coffee shop. They can be reviewed and amended over time but it will give everyone, especially new team members, clarity of what is expected of them.

You may think that simple and obvious things don't need to be included, but what is obvious to you may not always be obvious to another person. Some examples of ground rules are:

- We will always be ready to work at the beginning of our shift.
- We will never say something about another team member that we would not say to their face.
- We will be fair with each other and support each other when needed, swapping shifts, covering absence and caring for each other.

- We will always leave the sections we are working in clean and fully stocked for the next shift
- When it's quiet we will look for things that need doing.

The head barista

This is such an important role it must not be overlooked. A coffee shop that is passionate about its product should have a head barista who is a real expert and has fantastic passion for the drinks. It's this person's responsibility to train the team, develop new drinks for the menu and be the guardian of quality in your coffee shop. This could be you, but the quicker you train somebody to take over from you in this role, then the quicker you will have fantastic coffee and drinks served all day every day, even when you're not there. The knowledge and training you give your team will make them proud of every drink they serve to your guests.

There are training bodies and courses available to help you with this. Your coffee supplier may even have a trainer who can support you. Two organisations that have many resources are The Specialty Coffee Association of Europe (SCAE) and The Beverage Standards Association (BSA).

The team members

Full time versus part time

We have always had the majority of full-time members in our team, with one or two part-timers to add flexibility. The main reason for this is that you want your team to focus on your business and not have them working a number of other jobs as well. Remember if someone is working part-time, then their training will take longer because of the number of days they are available in the business to learn. They might never be as efficient as a full-time member of the team and there isn't really a place in a coffee bar for somebody to just clear tables. There will be a time when you need that person to work behind the bar, so everybody needs to be multi-skilled and able to work everywhere.

The trading pattern of your coffee shop will also dictate the ratio of full time versus part time. If you have a very busy weekend trade like many coffee shops, taking up to 70% of the trade on Friday, Saturday and Sunday, then you will need the flexibility of part timers.

Recruiting criteria

- Naturally happy positive people will make your business a happy friendly place. Do they have a happy resting face, i.e. do they look happy even when they are not trying.

- Do they have a reference? If so contact their previous employer. TIP- Do this while they are on their trial shift. When talking to past employers don't ask if they were any good, as even if they weren't you won't get a straight answer. Instead just say 'I'm ringing about, they seem great', the reaction you get will usually be an honest one!

- Do they have a spring in their step? Do they walk fast or slow? TIP- Ask them to follow you somewhere and walk very fast, do they keep up with you?

- Do they have any relevant experience? Experience is nice but their attitude is key.

You can teach the skills to become a barista, but you can't teach someone to emotionally engage and interact. Danny Mayer, in his book 'Setting The Table' (Mayer), introduces us to the concept of Enlightened Hospitality, where he emphasises putting the power of hospitality to work in a new and counterintuitive way.

Employment law changes and is different in different areas of the world, so you must ensure you comply with your local regulations. Many business organisations such as The Federation of Small

Businesses (FSB) can provide you with everything you need in terms of application forms, contracts and disciplinary procedures. Get this right from day one otherwise you will get into difficulty.

If or when an employee tries to take you to an employment tribunal it will be too late to realise that you are not complying with the law.

Set clear job descriptions, roles and responsibilities for each job
Every successful business needs the right balance between rules and empowerment. People like to know what they are responsible and accountable for. Without that clarity it is very difficult for the manager to review their performance and set them improvement targets. So having clear job descriptions and rules and responsibilities is essential.

A simple way to do this is to think about what you, as the owner would want everyone to do when they are working in a certain role. Write down the five or six key things that you would expect from a member of the team, which will make your business run well. These would be non-negotiable.

For example, you would expect the person on the till to:

- Offer a warm friendly welcome to every guest
- Take the orders accurately

- Always try to upsell appropriately
- Ensure that the guests are members of your loyalty scheme
- Communicate the orders to the rest of the team clearly
- Make no mistakes on the till

Do this for every position or role in your business and you will soon have a standard that you can train to and review against. If you do this yourself, it will be full of your values and nobody else's.

Before we did this ourselves, we asked our team to do the same thing. They wrote down what they thought their jobs were. Interestingly, there was a massive difference between what they thought they should do and what we as the business owner wanted them to do; for example the person on the till thought their job was just to take the money.

Taking the time to do this is critical. Many small business owners don't think about things like this and when they get started they don't have the time.

Always give new starters trial shifts

Assess them on the following criteria:

- Do they look for things to do?
- Do they interact with guests well?

- Have they got a sixth sense when it comes to reading guests needs?
- Do they pick things up quickly?
- Do they interact with the team well?
- Are they confident?
- How do they react under pressure?
- Do they ask questions?
- Do they smile and make eye contact?

Always employ on a trial period, with agreed dates for reviews. By giving them a handbook and job description, it makes it very easy to review the new starter against the criteria. They will know what they need to do to improve and you will know what training and support you need to give to get them there.

Team handbook

Your team handbook should cover the following:

- Your story
- Your values and principles
- Health and safety training
- Guest service
- Emergency procedures

- Ground rules
- Uniform guidelines
- Attendance policy
- Coffee knowledge and history
- Anything you want to focus on in your business

Once you have compiled your team handbook, which is continually being updated, ensure that each team member is given this on day one. They must use this resource to ensure their knowledge and quality of service meets your standards.

This forms part of their terms and conditions of employment, so you need to ensure that it is all legally compliant. We recommend that you join the Federation of Small Businesses (FSB), as soon as you set up your business. The FSB will be able to provide free legal advice and many other benefits that you will undoubtedly need.

Culture and management style

The culture will be driven by your values and your style of management. If you have a great set of values but don't manage your people to them, then that is a recipe for disaster.

Contrary to popular belief most people perform better when there is both a structure and freedom to make decisions in an organisation.

So having clear rules, responsibilities, and targets are really important.

The following diagram shows that there are four types of workplace; the best performing businesses are always in segment 1.

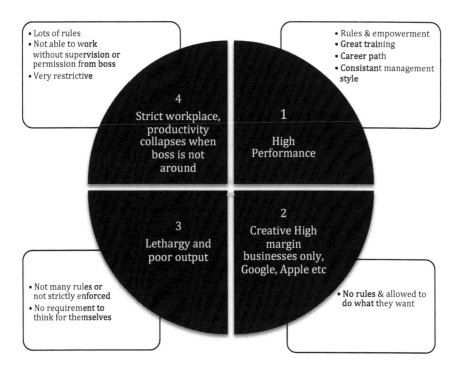

How to recruit a great team

This is one of the most frequent questions we get asked. There is no one factor that will deliver this but a combination of many:

- Always be recruiting - always be on the look out for great people, even if you have no vacancies at the moment. Take the time to talk to potential employees when they approach you about a job and keep hold of their details.
- Become a magnet business - if your business is a great place to work, where the existing team is happy and people have fun, word will get out and more people will approach you.
- Gum Tree is a bad idea - as from our experience, you get poor quality applicants that end up wasting your time.
- Don't forget your window - have a recruitment sign up permanently.
- Use social media - Facebook and Twitter have proved very successful. Facebook advertising is very targeted but can be expensive, so needs to be controlled.
- Don't employ temporary team members- by the time you train them and they get to know your guests, they will be on their way.
- Offer decent sized shifts- unless shorter shifts fit in with the person's circumstances.

Communication

A team will not be effective unless there is great communication in the team. Ideas to help you achieve this are:

- Set up a private Facebook group to communicate.
- Have a white board near the serving area, for messages and targets for that day.
- Agree a weekly team talk to discuss the week's priorities.
- A shift briefing before the start of every shift.
- Have monthly full team meetings.
- Publically display the objectives and targets and let people know how the business is doing.

Regular reviews

There is nothing better for building a great team than investing your time on a one to one with each member of the team.

A review should not take too long; about half an hour is ideal. The team member being reviewed and the reviewer need to prepare for the review by filling in a few details about what they are doing well, and what they need more support in. Also include what they feel good about and anything they are worried about.

Keeping a record of your reviews is very important; we use a simple word template. You can download a copy at www.dailygrindbook.com/resources

Holiday management

If you don't have clear rules and a stringent process for managing holidays, you will get into serious trouble running your business effectively and efficiently. This will impact on your ability to provide great guest service and will also affect your cash flow, as you will have to pay for two people, instead of one.

With a small team, having more than one person off at a time will cause you pain, especially if something unexpected happens, as it is likely to due to 'Murphy's Law!' (If it can go wrong, it will go wrong and at the worst possible time). During our first Christmas we had two sisters working for us, who begged us for time off to go home for two weeks over Christmas and New Year. We naively agreed. One other member of the team was disgruntled about this, but otherwise it didn't look as if it would cause any issues, as we employed seven people in total. Then unexpectedly two things happened. On Christmas Eve one of the team was involved in a car crash, and was signed off with whiplash for two weeks, so we were down to four. Then a wave of flu hit the team and suddenly we were down to three people to cover the busy Christmas trading period.

The only option was for us to work over the whole period all day, every day. Since then we have adopted the following rules:

- Holidays must be agreed with the manager before they are booked
- Only one person can be off at any one time
- Holidays are to be taken from Monday to Sunday, so only cover one weekend
- No holidays can be taken in December
- Holidays can't be carried over between years
- The manager can't have holidays at the same time as the owner

You can agree your own set of rules depending on the location and trading pattern of your business, but it's important to set these rules down early. The accepted norm in hospitality is that bank holidays are treated like any other day, so your team will be allowed twenty-eight days holiday per year if they work full time. You need to plan these carefully, as it has a big impact on your service levels and wage bill. Most people will look at having a week in autumn and winter, and two weeks in the summer. This will leave them with, eight odd days to book off over the year. The last thing you want is to have everyone trying to cram their holidays into the last few weeks of the holiday calendar, so plan them carefully. Be careful of the rules around what you can pay as holiday pay, as it's quite complicated.

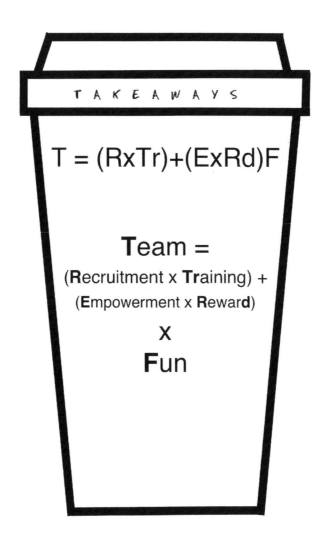

WOW Service

Every owner says that they want to give the best service possible in their coffee shop or café, and they all know that not providing excellent service is a sure fire way to close your business fast!

Fantastic service should be at the core of any hospitality business and be a central part of the values you have described earlier.

Service is also about the environment as well. The music, the smell, the signage, the lighting and your website, all support that first impression that your guest will receive. First impressions are the lasting ones.

Having clear service standards is a key element in getting your service right from the day your doors open.

Disney has some of the best customer service in the world. Here are the Disney service guidelines as they are a good place to start:

- Make eye contact and smile
- Greet and welcome each and every guest
- Seek out guest contact
- Provide immediate service recovery
- Display appropriate body language at all times

- Preserve the 'Magical' guest experience
- Thank each and every guest

It all starts with you and how you behave. How your manager behaves and your team behaves will all be affected by you. The old saying, 'behaviour breeds behaviour' is so true in our business.

The team

The leader of the team must set the right culture and recruit the best people. Employing people who have a natural smile and energy about them, then training them well, is a great start.

What you will find as well is that when you have a great atmosphere in your business, this will act like a magnet to good people when you want to recruit. Great team players like working with similar types of personalities, so if you have a great friendly team they will attract like-minded people. Watch out if you employ grumpy people, as you will have a queue of them waiting to join you!

It's always worth remembering at this point the lifetime value of your guests. Someone spending £5 per day, five days a week, fifty weeks a year, over ten years is worth £12,500.

If you can get your team to imagine that every guest has £12,500 tattooed on his or her forehead, then nothing would be too much trouble.

Types of guests

Raving fans: These are your ultimate loyal guests. They tell everyone how great you are and could even be part of your marketing team!

Delighted guests/loyal guests: Ask yourself would you like a loyal or regular boyfriend or girlfriend? You can see straight away the difference between them. To get delighted guests you just need to exceed what you promised by any amount, no matter how small;

Delight = Expectation +1

Disney call this 'plussing the show', where they constantly look for ways to improve the guest experience.

A delighted guest will also stay loyal even if there is a problem in the future.

Satisfied/regular guests: When you provide what they expect then they are satisfied but will not be loyal and are likely to visit less frequently than a loyal guest.

Dissatisfied guests: When you do less than what you promise, people are dissatisfied; they stop buying, tell ten people how bad you are, usually exaggerating the problem and don't come back. Most of these guests don't complain and allow you to rectify the situation because they are embarrassed. They fear problems in the future.

Get you back guests: These are the dissatisfied guests with attitude. They will post bad reviews on social media and try to tell everyone how bad you are.

How we lose guests

- 1% die
- 3% move away
- 4% are natural floaters
- 5% move to another coffee shop on recommendation
- 9% find somewhere cheaper
- 10% chronic complainers and leave
- 68% go elsewhere because the people who serve them are indifferent to their needs

Dealing with guest complaints

Dealing with complaints is such an important point that you need a process in place and to ensure that your team are trained well to deal with this inevitability.

We find that because of the passion that the barista have for the quality of their drinks, that it is too easy for them to take any complaint as personal, and react accordingly. It is critical that they understand that another person's opinion on their work is just that and remember that their ultimate job is to make the guest happy.

Here is a summary of what you should ensure your team do to deal with complaints well:

- Take full responsibility for the complaint even if you have nothing to do with it
- Use non-aggressive behaviour
- Listen
- Summarise
- Empathise
- Offer a solution
- Never take it personally

The guest is not always right, but deserves to be listened to.

A letter from an anonymous guest

I am your guest

You often accuse me of carrying a chip on my shoulder, but I suspect this is because you do not entirely understand me. Isn't it normal to expect satisfaction for one's money spent? Ignore my wants and I will no longer appear in your restaurant. Satisfy those wants and I will become increasingly loyal. Add a little extra personal attention and a friendly touch and I will become a walking advertisement for you.

When I criticize your food and service to anyone who will listen, which I may do whenever I am displeased, take heed. I am not dreaming up displeasure. It lies in something I perceive you have failed to do to make my eating experience as enjoyable as I have anticipated. Eliminate that perception or you will lose my friends and me as well. I insist on the right to dine leisurely or eat in haste according to my mood.

I refuse to be rushed, as I abhor waiting. This is an important privilege that my money buys. If I am not spending big money this particular time, just remember, if you treat me right I will return with a larger appetite, more money and probably with my friends.

I am much more sophisticated these days than I was just a few years ago. I've grown accustomed to better things and my needs are more complex. I'm perfectly willing to spend, but I insist on quality to match prices. I am above all, a human being. I am especially sensitive when I am spending money. I can't stand to be snubbed, ignored or looked down upon.

Whatever my personal habits may be, you can be sure that I'm a real nut on cleanliness in restaurants. Where food is concerned I demand the strictest sanitation measures. I want my meals handled and served by the neatest of people and in sparkling clean dishes. If I see dirty fingernails, cracked dishes or soiled table clothes you won't see me again.

You must prove to me again and again that I have made a wise choice in selecting your restaurant above others. You must convince me repeatedly that being a restaurant guest is a desirable thing in the first place. I can, after all, eat at home. So, you must provide something extra in food and service. Something so superior it will beckon me from my own table to yours.

Do we understand each other?

- Author unknown

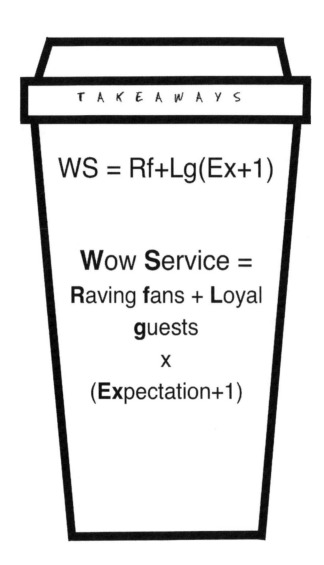

TAKEAWAYS

$$WS = Rf+Lg(Ex+1)$$

Wow **S**ervice =
Raving **f**ans + **L**oyal
guests
x
(**Ex**pectation+1)

What Products Will You Sell?

The whole area of what you sell should reflect and be informed by your core values. Whether it is fair trade, direct trade or neither. Are you going to support your local suppliers? Is it going to be the best, the biggest, the tastiest, the freshest or the trendiest? You should always have a back-story to help with your marketing, which will add value to everything you sell.

It's all about positioning and value proposition. In other words how your product compares to other similar products and where it sits in your range.

Think of designer handbags. To make the standard handbag of the range seem great value at a thousand pounds, the manufacturers produce an exclusive handbag for ten thousand pounds. Although only a few of the highest priced handbags are sold, their existence convinces the buyer that a thousand pounds is a reasonable price to pay for a designer handbag.

The products we sell are not in the hundreds of pounds I know, but the principle is the same. The way to differentiate your products versus a competitor is to have a little story for every product. Here are some examples that might help you:

- All cakes made here by Stacey!
- All our milk is organic
- We bake our pastries fresh every day
- Our baristas have all achieved level five training standards

You need to tell you own story as well. Guests love to support independent businesses and they really love getting to know the people behind the business too.

The variety of your range is important. Research constantly tells us that regular guests get bored with the same products very quickly and a regularly changing menu is a reason that guests say they visit an establishment. Changing your menu too regularly however will alienate people, so a happy medium of having a core range and changing a few items regularly in line with the seasons, is a good compromise.

When building your range consider the following guidelines:

- Split your menu into breakfast/lunch/afternoon/evening
- Have high, medium and lower priced products in a similar product group, so that people are encouraged to trade up
- Try to have no more than three of each flavour or type

- When considering drink sizes, it is useful to know that a three size range of drinks will give you 8% more revenue than a two size drink range
- Think about offering products of different quality and classify them as good, better and best
- Is there a natural up sell or complementary product that works well together?
- Add two or three products together to make a different product, e.g. a scone and tea, to make a cream tea
- Ensure products can they be taken away easily
- Decide where products will be displayed best

There will be four types of products that make up your range; short life, long life, fast sellers and slow sellers.

The drinks range is the simplest to manage, as it will consist of mainly short life milk combined with longer life ingredients, such as coffee, chocolate, syrups and teas. You can have a massive range of drinks with all combinations of these ingredients with little risk of waste. The other drinks will be canned or bottled and have a long shelf life but have a lower profit and selling price so they should compliment the range of drinks you make yourself rather than compete.

If you decide to make sandwiches and other food items yourself use shorter life ingredients in multiple products. This will to reduce the overall number of ingredients you need to buy in which will keep the waste to a minimum and reduce the amount of storage space you will need.

When planning your range of food, try and get the right balance to meet you guests' needs for different parts of the day. Consider as well, if you have sufficient vegetarian, gluten free, healthy, halal and non-dairy options covered.

If you get the range wrong for your location, unless your mission in life is to educate guests and persuade them to buy your range, then it could potentially be a costly error.

The next step is to agree the core range that will change infrequently or just be tinkered with, rather then totally changed.

When you have chosen the core range then it's time to bring new lines in around the edges of the range, as specials or seasonal, to keep the whole range fresh in the eyes of your guests. If you decide to keep a new line as a core line, then it's good to stop selling another line. Otherwise you will soon be stocking too many products that will be difficult to manage logistically, incur higher wastage and potentially confuse guests.

Once you have agreed a range, the next step is to calculate the profit margins. The gross profit is the sales revenue minus the cost of goods sold. The net profit is the sales revenue minus all cost of goods, operating expenses, taxes and interest.

At this point it's worth mentioning the biggest source of confusion that people have when working out their profit margins.

They forget to include the VAT or tax element, and incorrectly calculate the profit as a multiple of the cost price. For example if a product costs £1 and sells for £4 then they wrongly calculate the profit as 300%.

So for example the table below explains how to calculate the gross profit of a £3.60 coffee:

Selling price	£3.60	
Net selling price	£3.00	= Selling price minus tax at 20%
Product cost	£1.00	
Gross profit	£2.00	= Net selling price minus product costs
Gross profit %	66.67%	= Gross profit divided by net selling price x 100

To make the business model for your new coffee shop work then you will need to achieve around 75% gross margin overall. To achieve this in a typical coffee shop with a typical sales mix of 65% drinks and 35% food, the drinks profit should be around 85% and the food profit around 70%. The more you make onsite, the higher the gross profit will be however you need to consider the extra work involved. We cover the benefits and costs of making products onsite versus buying in later in this chapter.

Everything you produce must be costed to the penny, including all ingredients and packaging. All products need their own recipe card or crib sheet for the team to follow. Without these procedures in place, you won't be able to deliver a consistent standard and maintain your gross profit.

The new regulations around allergens also mean that you will have to have a record of what allergens are included in every product you sell, available for guests to see.

Pricing

Setting your prices

Once you understand your profit margins then you can work out how much you can charge for products. Your range will be a mixture of known value items (KVI's) i.e. the commodity products that are widely available and similar to other coffee shops; latte, tea and muffins etc. and unique differentiated products. It's difficult to charge higher prices for the KVI's without giving the perception to guests that you are an expensive business. The trick is to differentiate enough of your KVI's to be unique enough that you can charge a higher price without being deemed as expensive.

You can add the unique element of the product through decoration, e.g. latte art and toppings, or through communication of the special properties of the product in its description and story. Often using an unusual price point ending in a 7 rather than a 9 can allow you to nudge the price up a little.

Putting together deals is a good way of getting guest to spend more, especially at quieter times; a breakfast deal with a drink and croissant or an afternoon tea deal. These should always be priced at about 75% more than your average spend per head to maximise the return. For example, if your average morning spend is £3, then put an offer together for £4.

As an independent, to try and compete with the chains on price effectively for the long term is folly. There will always be a competitor cheaper than you, who have deeper pockets and a better supply chain. As an independent your main weapons are; better friendlier service, being able to respond to guest demand almost instantly and good quality innovative local products.

Choosing your coffee

Arguably the most important decision you will make will be the type of coffee you serve. We could write a book on that alone. It will be your biggest cost after team wages. The key things to remember are:

There are a few ways you can get your coffee. An artisan roaster, a bespoke roaster, roast yourself, or off the shelf.

The artisan roaster will typically be a smaller business that has passion for coffee and will roast their own beans. They will have a number of different styles, typically source the coffee direct and have a few different blends. The things to watch here is the consistency of the roasting and the price because it's generally at the top end.

The artisan coffee can be four times the price of off the shelf coffee.

A bespoke roaster will be able to provide you with a blend that you like, to your specification, because they are more commercial in their set up. Their consistency in roasting will be excellent and they will also be able to brand your coffee for you. This is typically better value but the volumes you need to buy will be higher.

Roasting coffee beans yourself is very possible now. There are a lot of 2kg shop roasters available for around £10 to £15k. With this option you are in total control and your guests are treated to theatre. There is a great retail sales side added to your business by selling the bags of coffee. The downsides are that it will be like running two separate businesses in one. Also you will need great ventilation and possibly planning permission for extract fans, as the process creates lots of heat and dust. These costs need to be factored in as extras.

If you decide to buy off the shelf, find a coffee you like from a wholesaler or direct from a larger roaster and use that. The benefits are that it will be more cost effective and consistent, but the downside is that it will lack much of a story.

Remember even the best and most expensive coffee can easily be ruined by many factors; such as poorly trained baristas, incorrect extraction, using the wrong grinder setting, a poorly maintained coffee machine, incorrect milk techniques and poor storage of the roasted coffee All will have an effect on the final product.

Training is key in so many aspects of running a coffee shop but the one thing you must get right consistently is the quality of the coffee you serve. So the training of the baristas is very important. Your guests will appreciate a great barista; they will even start avoiding visiting when their favourite barista is not on shift.

Don't forget to consider serving filter coffee. It has become more popular and it's an easy way for you to experiment and add variety to your offer.

Some key points to consider when choosing your coffee:

- It must fit with your values
- It must be consistently roasted, otherwise you will constantly be changing the grinder setting
- Can the supplier train your team and keep you up to date with current trends
- Does the supplier close down for long periods of time?

Tea

Having a great tea offer is really important too; remember that in the UK there are twice as many cups of tea drunk than coffee.

If you want to be able to sell the tea at maximum profit, then selling in a teapot is mandatory. There is little perceived value of a tea bag in a cup. There is also the opportunity to sell the retail packs of the tea as well.

The minimum you will need to stock is a great breakfast tea, earl grey, decaf tea, and a few infusions. The shelf life and easy storability of teas allows you to stock a big range without risk of waste and without tying up much capital

There is currently a big movement towards loose-leaf teas. It's a good idea to have loose leaf for the more specialty teas of your range and keep the English breakfast tea as a tea bag, for ease of service and to build the value gap between the bags and the loose leaf.

Branded cups or plain

It's really easy to get your china or paper cups branded. There are a number of options but you need to look at your values before you decide which route to go down.

Branded cups make your business look professional and bigger than it is, which in turn makes your business look less like an independent.

Branded china cups or mugs can be reasonably priced.

Branded paper cups can be the same price as plain cups but the minimum orders to get a good price is high and you will be tying up a lot of capital. You'll also need lots of room to store the minimum 50 cases of each size.

A good compromise is to look for quirky, off the shelf china cups and combine them with plain disposable cups that you self stamp with a custom designed stamp.

If you decide to order branded cups, remember to factor in at least a twelve-week lead-time for deliveries.

Cup sizes and mugs versus cup & saucer

It depends on your target guest and style of service but we always recommend serving tea in teapots, with cups and saucers, rather than mugs. The cups and saucers can be used for other smaller sized drinks as well.

Having three sizes of cups will increase your sales overall by about 8% versus just having two sizes. More people will choose the middle size.

A typical independent will use 8oz, 12oz and 16oz mugs or cups, although chains use 12oz, 16oz and 20oz.

Seasonal fare

Sales of hot drinks tend to drop by 30% in the summer, so a coffee shop that does not try and combat this by adding a good range of iced teas and coffees, will find the summer months quiet.

You don't want to rely on selling just bottled or canned drinks, as the profit on these will be much lower than an iced drink you make. Developing a good range of iced drinks is easy. You need to have a few good quality blenders, as they will need to be long lasting and repairable. Also a good ice machine that is capable of making at least 50kg of ice a day. You will find that on a hot busy day your iced drinks will be 70% of your sales, so be prepared.

A selection of iced drinks could include:

- Iced coffee
- Iced teas
- Smoothies
- Shakes
- Frappes
- Ice-cream

Your food range will need to be adapted for the warmer months as well, so consider some lighter sandwiches and some salads.

Equally, you need to adapt your menu for the colder months. With hot chocolate and comfort foods such as soup.

Seasonal events such as Christmas and Easter as well as celebration days like Mothers Day or Halloween, will give you an opportunity to do something different. You can customise an existing product like a cupcake or a hot chocolate to add some theatre to your range.

The merchandising layout

When planning your merchandising layout consider your guests' journey through your business. Starting outside, what can they see through the window that would tell them what you do? When they walk in, what do they see? Is it obvious where to stand to be served and are products merchandised together so guests can make a decision easily, e.g. bottle drinks near sandwiches. People take about five seconds to make up their minds and if they can't easily see a product they might not spend extra time looking for it.

Knowing where they can order and where they can wait for the drinks are important factors in making your guests feel at ease. This prevents confusion and potential upset when guests collect the wrong drinks.

What they have on their table and what they can see on the walls around them will influence them to come back and spend more so having information about your business on display will engage your guests.

Labelling your products

Clear pricing and good description on product labels are very important and often overlooked by the independent business. It can make the difference between people buying what they know or buying what interests them, which will often be at a higher price. Don't use currency symbols on any label or menu, as its been proven that sales increase if they are omitted.

Have a product benefit on the label as well as the product description; such as freshly baked or vegetarian etc.

Not having clear labelling and pricing will slow down sales, particularly impulse sales as people are afraid of 'bill shock' at the till if they don't know how much it costs when they pick it up off the shelf. Many people have a mental budget for their needs or snack and won't want to go over that.

Upsells

How many times have you walked into a shop for something and walked out with two or three extra items that go with the original item. It should be the same for your coffee shop, encouraging guests to buy additional complementary items they didn't intend buying, would have a big impact on your sales.

Two easy ways of upselling are using complementary merchandising, i.e. having two things that would normally be apart in the shop that go together and putting them side by side. Or impulse merchandising, i.e. having mints or bottled water by the till. This will have a big impact on your sales.

Other ideas are; selling a lunch item to someone that comes in for breakfast, by the team making suggestions for later, or encouraging guests to come in later by issuing a voucher to be used at their next visit.

You need to consider changing the impulse buys at the till to reflect different times of the day. Having a breakfast item at the till in the morning and a cookie in the afternoon, for example, will tempt guests who would otherwise just buy what they came in for, to spend more.

Of course the simplest and easiest way, that has the single biggest effect on what people buy, is what the person on the till recommends to them. Having a clever script for team members taking the order or taking the money will pay dividends.

The amount of times we hear when ordering in other coffee shops the team member asking, after the initial order, 'anything else?' is astonishing. This does nothing to try and get you to buy more and is very lazy. It's a closed question that normally gets answered with no.

We have clear rules for this at the till. We train the team to try and put themselves in the guests shoes and guess what they might like and then offer that to them in a way that will get them salivating for it. Examples are:

- 'Can I tempt you with a croissant? They have just come out of the oven and are still warm.'
- 'How about a freshly baked muffin this afternoon? It's Friday so calories don't count!'

When taking the order for drinks always default to a bigger size first. The chains never offer a small size of anything, and they always offer syrup, cream or extra topping. You can do the same.

Make and bake versus buy in

When you are planning your range you will need to decide how much of your range you make yourself, bake yourself or buy in.

It depends on your values but more practically on the available space and skill level in the business. Whatever you decide, you must ensure that you can do things consistently, both in terms of quality and in terms of profit.

On initial consideration, you would think that making everything yourself would be the way to get the best profit and the freshest possible product. However, when calculating your profit with buy-in versus made on site, you need to weigh up the following issues. Making yourself on site has a potential higher profit but consider the additional costs which include, the team time, extra equipment and energy costs. Also remember possible waste through the production process, by having inconsistent results. You will also need extra storage for ingredients as to get the best prices you will need to buy in bulk.

We have tried different approaches over the years and you must do what is right by your values without it causing a major operational issue for you.

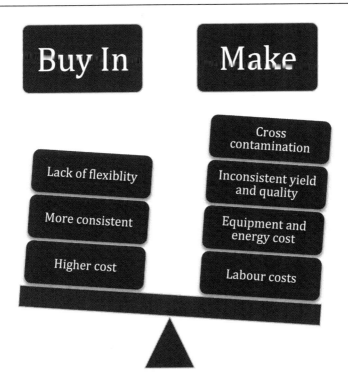

Food intolerances

You will be aware of the allergens regulations that came into force in 2015. There are currently fourteen different allergens that you need to identify. Either indicate these on the packaging label or have the information to hand to tell guests when they enquire for loose, unpackaged or items made and sold on site. The fourteen allergens that you need to advise guests of are:

1. Cereals
2. Crustaceans

3. Eggs

4. Fish

5. Peanuts

6. Soybeans

7. Milk (Including Lactose)

8. Nuts

9. Celery

10. Mustard

11. Sesame seeds

12. Sulphur dioxide (>10mg/kg or 10g/l)

13. Lupin

14. Mollusc

You will need to put together a matrix of everything you sell that is not sold in manufacturer labelled packaging. It is not as arduous as you might think, as your suppliers will be able to send you a list of everything they sell. Here is an example, which also can be found at www.dailygrindbook.com/resources

Product	Celery/Celeriac	Cereals Containing Gluten	Crustaceans	Egg	Fish	Lupin	Milk	Molluscs	Mustard	Nuts	Peanuts	Sesame	Soya	Sulphites (Sulphur Dioxide)
Bacon Roll		Y												
Ketchup	Y													
Brown Sauce		Y												
Cheese & Tomato Roll		Y					Y							
Mushroom Roll		Y												
Ham & Cheese Croissant		Y		Y			Y			May Contain			May Contain	
Cheese & Tomato Croissant		Y		Y			Y			May Contain		Y	May Contain	
Yoghurt Pot		Y					Y						Y	
Toast		Y												
porridge		Y					Y							
granola pot		Y					Y					Y		
Mozzarella & Tomato Panini		Y		Y			May Contain		Y			May Contain		
Spicy Meatball Panini		Y					Y		Y			May Contain		
Brie & Bacon Panini		Y					Y					May Contain		
HAM & CHEESE PANINI		Y					Y		Y			May Contain		
Sausage Toastie		Y					Y						Y	Y
Ham & Cheese Toastie		Y					Y						Y	
Cheese & Tomato Toastie		Y					Y						Y	
Egg Mayo sandwich		Y		Y			Y		Y				Y	
Cheddar & Caramelised onions		Y					Y		Y				Y	
Ham Salad		Y					Y						Y	
chicken & Avocado														

There is a great marketing opportunity here as well, as one in five people in the UK think they have some type of food intolerance. So that person in a party of people, will be the one who is going to have the strongest opinion on where they are going to eat.

Those businesses that have a have a range of products or are able to adapt their menu, to provide gluten or lactose free and a vegetarian or vegan option, will prosper.

T A K E A W A Y S

GP = (Co+St+Ca)Pt

Great **P**roducts =
(**Co**nsistancy + **St**ory +
Care)
x
Prof**it**

The Importance Of A Good Layout and Design For Your New Coffee Shop

Size

A good size for a coffee shop is about 1500 ft² to 2000 ft², anything smaller and you won't be able to get enough seats in, to take enough money to break even. Before you sign any lease or agreement, you need to consider whether you will be able to fit all the equipment and facilities in without compromising the guest space.

If you haven't done anything like this before, then it's worth speaking to an expert and getting their advice and perhaps a draft plan drawn up. This will help you out at a later stage anyway when you talk to your builder. It will also identify if there are any hidden costs, such as moving of electrical supply or issues with ventilation, plumbing or drainage. This will save you money in the long term.

Check you have enough power to the distribution board to supply sufficient power for your equipment, that the hot water tank is big enough for your needs and that there is a place for the ventilation and all the air conditioning units.

Consider the guest flow through the building and importantly the working practices of the production of food and coffee as well as the washing up area.

Making a mistake at this point will cost you dearly for the whole life of your business. Having things in the wrong place, too far apart or not enough room between them to actually work, have a very negative effect on the productivity of your team, the speed at which they are able to work and the number of people able to work in any one area at one time.

Equipment layout

Planning locations of ovens, dishwashers, coffee machines, sinks, production areas and storage areas is critical. Think about where you will serve the coffee from and where to wash the dishes. Draw plans of the layout of the equipment and visualise how the layout will work. You don't want the dishwashing area in full view of the guest, as this will always look messy, but you will need it in the right place for productivity, so that the team aren't falling over themselves. You need enough room behind the counter to be able to work safely and productively, however not at the detriment of the space needed for guests and seating. Think and plan very carefully at this stage, as a mistake will be very costly. Don't make hasty decisions and have different layout plans to choose from. Remember that your builder may prefer a certain layout because it is easier for him to fit out, but always choose the layout that works best for you.

It's worth looking at spending some time analysing how the big chains layout their interiors. They spend many millions of pounds reviewing and adjusting the look and feel of their businesses because they know that small changes have a great impact on their profit.

The coffee shop is full of things that generate heat and moisture so having good ventilation is critical. Guests won't stay for very long if it's too hot or humid. When you look at new coffee shops you will see that most of them forget this vital issue. When the summer arrives they have electric fans everywhere, the team are complaining and the place is empty. Then in the winter the windows are steamed up and you can't see in or out.

Guest toilets are important; although in some cases is not a legal requirement. Having good facilities will bring more guests to your coffee shop. The other thing to consider is level access through the doors; they need to be wide enough for a pushchair and for a wheelchair.

Think about your prospective guest avatar and consider what sort of space they would like. Try and build the different areas into your layout plan:

- Do you need quiet areas, high tables or low tables?

- How long will your guest avatar wish to stay?

- Will they need plug sockets to charge laptops?

- Will they want a combination of low comfortable seating and tall tables and chairs to work?

- Will they choose to sit at communal tables or private areas where conversations cannot be overheard?

- Will your seating area be multifunctional, so that it can be rearranged if a larger group arrives?

- Will you have baby highchairs to attract families and have room to fit the highchair at the table?

Wear and tear

Serviceability of equipment is vital. Think how the seats will look after coffee has been spilt over them; are they easy to clean or will they look dirty and uninviting. Think how serviceable the colour of the material is, as some will show the dirt more than others and some materials will last longer.

Choose the flooring wisely. It has to be easy to clean and durable. Some show every mark and others are more camouflaging. If you're going for the latest trends, remember they will be out of date very quickly.

Lighting is essential so plan carefully. Do you want a bright vibrant area or a calm chilled area? Do you want to open during the evening and be able to dim lighting to change the atmosphere? Whatever lighting you choose; remember to have low energy bulbs.

Design

So choose your design carefully. You can employ designers but keep a close eye on costs and have a fixed budget. Some designers will complete just the plans for you, so that you become the project manager and save money. But factor in the time it will take to complete, including the lost revenue of putting back the opening date, if work isn't completed on time. If you decide to design yourself, do your research. Have a look at the competition locally and in major cities, and at the cutting edge new designs.

Make up a vision board of the different aspects you like, as this will help to get to your final design. Do you have an eye for design or should you delegate? Remember, fashion changes constantly and so your fabulously designed coffee shop may become out of date very quickly.

There are lots of resources available on Pinterest that will help you with ideas. The chances are though, that you have an idea of what you want your coffee shop to look and feel like as soon as you have agreed your values.

A good design will pay itself back many times over. The coffee shop business is not all about great coffee; it's about the third space. Starbucks calls it; a home from home, an office, a meeting room and a chill out space. If people like your space and it suits their need, they will visit more often.

There are a number of key things to consider when planning the layout.

Remember you need space for guest moving and queuing, through the coffee shop and at the till. The guests' journey through the space should be intuitive. Where to select from, queue, pay and collect the drinks is important, so that the new guest feels at home. These areas should be instantly recognisable to them, as most coffee shops get a lot of walk in trade.

Don't have seats too close to the counter and have room for the order line and the people collecting drinks to walk past. Remember people will move furniture around to suit their own needs as well.

Zones

You need different types of zones for different times of day, types of guests and quantity of guests. Have at least three different types of zones to make the place enticing for your guests:

- A place to work or have a meeting with higher tables, plug sockets and some privacy. Perhaps towards the back of the coffee shop.
- Areas to just relax, read the paper and watch the world go by, with lower softer chairs providing a good view of what's going on.
- Somewhere where you can sit on your own but not feel alone, for example in the window on tall chairs is a good place.

Tables and displays

There is currently a fashion for sharing tables. In our experience these work well in large spaces but are normally the last seats to fill up. The table size you choose will control the number of guests you can seat at any one time. Your guests will mainly arrive in ones and twos, so large tables with only one or two guests occupying them will give the appearance that the coffee shop is full. This will discourage others guests from coming in. We recommend square tables seating two, as a good option for coffee shops with limited space as these can easily be moved together by guests in bigger parties. Round tables can't be adapted as easily so should be used for low tables with soft seating preferably.

Your food menu also dictates the table size. If you are serving light snacks and drinks then a 600mm or even 500mm table will suffice. If your menu is more extensive, then you may need bigger tables.

Wobbly tables are the scourge of coffee shops and restaurants the world over. Three legged tables and tables with round table bases don't wobble.

You will also need room for your team and storage. Work backwards from your peak time to work out how many people will be on each shift and if they will all be able to work safely and efficiently in the space you allot them. Consider where you will store the key items you need during a busy shift; milk, paper cups, bins etc. These areas need serious consideration and time spent on planning, as getting this wrong at this stage will cost you a lot of money every day through poor productivity.

People buy with their eyes; so enticing displays are important and congruent images displayed on the walls and near the point of sale will increase the amount people spend. Merchandising complementary products close by and in a logical order will also make it easier for people to upsell themselves. If you want to see what works visit a Starbucks and look at the items that are merchandised by the till. They will be there because the analysis shows that they add the greatest profit.

A word of caution, the coffee shops with the quirkiest or cutting edge designs don't necessarily make money.

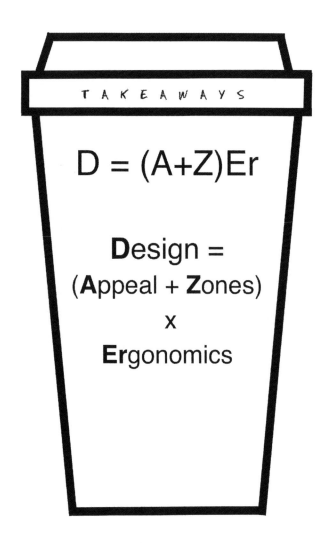

TAKEAWAYS

$$D = (A+Z)Er$$

Design =
(**A**ppeal + **Z**ones)
x
Ergonomics

<u>Equipment</u>

Service contracts

One thing a coffee shop owner must invest in is a good coffee machine and grinders. A coffee shop will never make money if their coffee machine breaks down. We recommend having a seven-day comprehensive service contract in place, to be able to call an engineer out as soon as the problem occurs. This contract will service the grinders and coffee machine, including boiler checks. You will never have a consistent coffee if your grinders and coffee machine aren't calibrated and serviced regularly. We believe this service contract is an essential investment.

How do you choose your coffee machine?

One thing that is certain is that there is no shortage of different makes, models and suppliers happy to tell you that their machine is the one you should buy. We counted forty-five different makes at the recent Caffè Culture Show at Olympia, where coffee equipment suppliers all come together every year. Choosing the right machine is a big decision and one that could have lasting consequences for your business.

The level of complexity of the modern coffee machine is amazing. There are machines that will weigh the shot as it is poured, adjust the temperature of the water at three different points, vary the pressure at the touch of a button and have multiple boilers all so you can make that elusive perfect shot.

There are different colours, designs and machines with varying numbers of heads, steam knobs or levers. You can have retro looking or sleek modern machines, that are, Italian, British, Spanish, French or Chinese.

You can buy machines new, second hand, reconditioned or leased, and you may be able to get one free from your coffee supplier. You can choose to have one or two machines, either bean to cup or traditional espresso. The choices just keep on coming.

When people ask why we chose our machines the answer was simple. We had a great relationship with our maintenance company and they recommended the machine they imported, as it was a good machine and they were able to service it quickly because they carried all the necessary parts.

When choosing a machine consider the following points:

Work out when your busiest hour will be and how many drinks you will need to make in that busiest time, and then match that to the capability of the machine. The general way that manufacturers describe the capacity of their machines is in cups per day. This is a pretty poor measure as most of a coffee shops demand will come in waves and not be a constant flow.

So a better way of calculating this is to use this rule of thumb. A one or two head machine would be ok for thirty cups per hour, but for anything more than that you will need a three head machine with two steam wands, so that two people can operate it at the same time.

You will need your machine to be automatic as well, so that you can calibrate the shot timings. Some machines are still manual and rely on you starting and stopping the shot, which when you are busy will be a big issue.

Have a high head machine and you will be able to get the cup underneath the shot, not just a shot glass, and will therefore save time.

Reliability of your machine will be essential, as you can't run a coffee shop without coffee, so speak to other owners of the machine about reliability.

We would NEVER consider buying a second hand machine unless it came with the same warranty as a new machine, it was from a reputable dealer and had been fully reconditioned. Do not buy from an auction or eBay unless you want trouble.

Without a water filter your machine will scale up and breakdown very quickly. So make sure your water hardness is measured and an appropriate size filter is added and ensure that it is changed as soon as it is spent.

Dishwasher

Invest in a good quality commercial dishwasher. We have known coffee shops that have cut corners and have bought cheap commercial dishwashers or even bought a domestic one. Big mistake! A domestic dishwasher will take a couple of hours to clean your dishes as opposed to a commercial dishwasher taking minutes. This results in washing by hand and not cleaning properly. Make sure you buy one with a drain pump and check the power requirements. Generally they require a 20amp supply.

Ovens

If you plan to bake off your own pastries and rolls, which we highly recommend you do, you will need a small bake off oven. Some suppliers offer them as an inducement to take their products but beware of the on-going higher prices of continuing to buy their products that will bring! Otherwise because they are fairly simple pieces of kit, it's something you could get second hand.

Panini grill or speed cook oven?

Depending on your product range you will need something to heat up food to order. If you are planning on a range of mostly paninis and toasties then a flat grill will do. If you want to be able to do a wider range then you need to consider a speed cook oven such as the Merry-chef or Turbo-chef range. Not only will these ovens speed up the service, cutting the time to heat a panini from four minutes on a flat grill to one minute with a speed cook oven, they will allow you to sell jacket potatoes, pies, pizzas and other open topped toasted products. In fact there is very little limit to what you can cook in these ovens.

The speed cooking ovens are more expensive to buy but the same to run as a flat grill. They will improve your service though, as guests will be able to collect everything from the counter and you won't need to deliver food to their tables later when you have a queue. Speed cook ovens may use 3-phase power so check this out first with your electrician.

Refrigeration

You will need a reasonable amount of fridges, both for display and storage.

A typical coffee shop will need a minimum of:

- A display fridge for self-service food and cold drinks
- A counter display fridge for cakes
- An under counter milk fridge near the coffee machine
- Two big upright storage fridges
- An upright or chest freezer

There are a lot of reputable sellers of second hand refrigeration and we would always consider using them. Check that the gas used in the refrigeration is legally compliant and the unit can be serviced!

Tables and chairs

This is a big decision, which depends on the style and design of your coffee shop. The amount of soft seating versus standard tables and chairs will depend on the size of your unit. Soft furnishings take up more space so will limit your capacity.

Whatever you choose, remember that they will need to be robust, as they will need to last a long time in a high wear environment. Choose your fabrics carefully!

Ventilation and air-conditioning

There is a lot of heat generated in a coffee shop, by the coffee machine, ovens, refrigeration and guests, so getting this right is crucial. People won't come in if it's too hot or cold. They also want to smell freshly make coffee and pastries, not the smell of cooking. We recommend taking professional advice with this as it's a bit of a science that you don't want to get wrong.

Maintenance and repairs

Find a local reliable contractor who will repair refrigeration units and dishwashers and deal with plumbing issues. Someone you can trust, who is quick to respond to a call out and is reliable.

You will become an expert odd job man in your business, saving thousands of pounds on repair bills. But you must weigh up the cost of your time compared with contracting out.

During our coffee life we have both become very good at DIY. When Andrew broke his collarbone skiing, Claire not only had to drive 721 miles home but also do both our jobs until he recovered.

Claire refurbished a toilet, plumbed in a hot water tap and fixed leaks to name but a few new skills learnt, even repairing the CCTV monitor!

A lot of equipment can be bought second hand, saving a lot of money. We kitted out one of our new sites with great second hand refrigeration equipment and saved £10k in the process. Choose carefully and wisely.

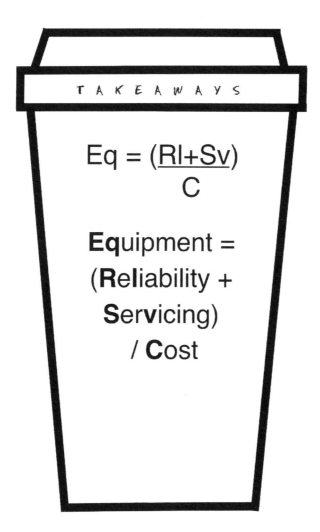

TAKEAWAYS

$$Eq = \frac{(Rl+Sv)}{C}$$

Equipment = (**Re**liability + **S**ervicing) / **C**ost

<u>Running Your Coffee Shop</u>

When people are asked why they choose a coffee shop, reliability is always in the top three reasons, alongside convenience and friendliness.

So what is reliability and how can you deliver it? Reliability is one of the big reasons why people visit chains because they know what they are going to get before they even walk through the door.

Michael Gerber in his book 'The E-Myth Revisited' (Gerber), gives an example of a barber he visited. The first time they washed his hair, stating that it gave a better cut, used only scissors and his coffee was topped up regularly. The second time he received no hair wash, they used a mixture of scissors and clippers and a glass of wine was offered. The third time, he again received no hair wash and a cup of coffee that wasn't topped up. Although each hair cut was excellent, because of the inconsistent nature of the service he no longer goes there.

It's the same with coffee shops. People want reliability and consistency. They want to know that their flat white will be as good tomorrow as it was today, that the cake will be as fresh and that the smile will be as welcoming.

One of the biggest issues that you come up against, time and time again in independent coffee shops, is the inconsistency of the drinks, if a less well-trained barista makes the drinks when the head barista is not there.

We have seen this happen in our businesses where guests will avoid visiting when their favourite barista is away, or always ask for their favourite barista to make their drinks. You might find this strange but the difference in a well-made coffee versus a poorly made one is so great that people become scared of ordering from someone they don't trust to make it for them.

So delivering consistency and reliability in everything you do is crucial for the long-term success of your business. So how do you deliver a consistent service day after day?

Good routines and systems plus great training.

Every process, routine & system should be documented. This should be done in such a way that even the newest, least experienced member of your team could understand what needs to be done and how to do it.

Before opening and in the first six weeks of opening, the routines and processes need to be reviewed and fine-tuned. In this way you will be able to deliver reliability to your guests even if you are not there.

This document gives you an added benefit of giving your team a structure to follow, with rules and timescales that will help them understand how well they are doing. It will help you immensely when you start to do performance reviews as well.

A great little tip that The Coffee Boys recommend in their book, 'Setting Up and Managing Your Own Coffee Bar' (Gilmartin & Richardson), is having a small notebook with you at all times. When something goes wrong and you need to retrain or fix a problem, you can write down what you do and record the training you give at that time. Use this as the basis for a new routine or to check that an existing routine or process is up to date.

As Michael Gerber describes in his book 'The E-Myth Revisited' (Gerber), *'Most new businesses are started by technicians -- people who are skilled at what they enjoy doing, and who figure they'd rather work for themselves than for someone else. It is a myth that new businesses are started by entrepreneurs.'*

A great position to come from is to imagine that your new coffee shop is going to be the first of a hundred more, even if you only want to have one coffee shop. By adapting this mind-set then you will put together systems and processes that will allow your team to learn how to run your business and deliver extraordinary results for you.

A common mistake in any independent business is to think that because you are independent, your team should be allowed to think for themselves and do things the way they want to do it, rather than the way you, the owner, knows works.

The great opportunity of running a small and agile business is being able to keep trying new ideas, benchmarking the ideas against the current way of doing things and quickly adopting the new better way. But be consistent so that everyone in your team does it the best way.

You will find that little changes in what you do can have a big impact, from the words you use when greeting a guest, to the position of a product in a display. Your job is to identify the best way and then ensure that everyone sticks to it.

There are lots of operational routines you need to set up in the business to keep you legal, compliant and consistent.

We suggest that you have the following in place:

Risk assessment

- Fire safety
- COSHH – Control of substances hazardous to health
- Equipment
- Pregnancy risk assessment
- Accident book
- Notice board signage
- Public liability insurance documents

Food safety

- Temperature records
- Cleaning routines and records
- Food safety training
- Allergens information

People

- Recruitment process – application forms and new starter forms
- Training records
- Team handbook
- Contract
- Disciplinary and grievance procedure
- Review documents

- Social media policy
- Mobile phone policy
- Smoking policy
- Ground rules

Operational routines

- Opening
- Closing
- Change over
- Cash up
- Banking
- Petty cash
- Ordering
- Delivery checking
- Claims procedures
- Deep cleaning
- Till training
- Recipes
- Waste and the team food recording
- Serving friends and family policy
- Discount and refunds policy
- Audits
- Stock taking

- Payroll
- Invoice management
- Bookkeeping
- Service standards

This is such an important topic and would likely fill another book. We have provided examples of these documents at www.dailygrindbook.com/resourses

Technology to help you run your business

There are many ways you can run your business more smoothly by using technology, some of which you can get for free. Here is a non-exhaustive list of resources we use to save us time and improve consistency.

LogMeIn

This is free and allows you to log in remotely to any computer you set up. You can log in on your smartphone or tablet as well. It's probably the most useful thing we use as we can solve most PC or cash up questions remotely. If you need more than the free connections then we have found Remote Utilities works well. It's very powerful but a little more complicated to set up.

Drop Box

This is also free to join and is a great way to collaborate or just work from anywhere using the latest version of your work. You can see your files on any device or computer and share selected files or folders with others. Be careful though as this is not a safe way to back up important information.

Facebook groups

Set up a private Facebook group for the team. You don't need to be friends on Facebook, but you can use it really well for communicating with your team regarding rotas, new lines, current offers, and what's happening etc.

Automatic mailing

We cover this much more in the Marketing Section, setting up a VIP club, but it can also be used to collect information for new starters and to set up templates to deal with guest complaints etc.

For example, we have set up a data capture page for new members of the team to fill in all their details before they start. We did this because there was always a query or a section not filled in correctly on the paper version, which slowed down the whole process. Now setting up a new starter is faster and more accurate. We have also used it to automate training and reviews.

Online accounts

Your accounting software should have an online dashboard and possibly an app to help you manage your invoicing and payments. We have always used Sage because that's what our accountant recommended. There is more choice now of online packages that will integrate with your bank. So do your homework and talk to your accountant.

Online banking

Use the online banking system your bank offers to download statements directly to your accounts package and to pay bills and manage your account.

Excel

Having knowledge of Excel is really helpful to help you analyse your numbers. It's worth doing some online tutorials to help with graphs and tables.

Gmail

It's unlikely that the email management software you get with your domain name will be as good as Gmail. You can link your own domain name to a Gmail account and have all the benefits of a Gmail account for storage and organisation of your emails. It's a little tricky to set up but your website host will be able to help you set it up. You also get the extra benefits of the G-drive for documents storage and sharing.

CCTV

CCTV is very cheap now and you should make sure you get a system that is accessible from anywhere via the Internet. Four camera systems are adequate for covering the till, office, counter and front door but eight or sixteen camera systems are not much more expensive. It's not big brother and you will benefit personally by knowing you can look in to your business 24/7 and that it will act as a deterrent to anyone wanting to steal from you or your guests. We would recommend that you get cameras everywhere you can and where possible have sound too.

I Auditor

This is a great app for your smart phone that has thousands of audits on and allows you to add your own.

Background burner

This is a great free tool to get rid of a background when you take a product shot. Just upload to the website and it will do all the hard work for you. Just remember to take a photo with an even contrasting background.

Wordswag

Use this tool to make great posters and signs that you can use on social media or anywhere you like.

YouTube

This is your complete training solution. If you want to find out about something, then it's on YouTube!

Back up drive/ personal cloud

A Network Attached Shared Drive or NAS drive will back up all your computers without you needing to worry. It can also be used for sharing files, like your very own drop box. Something simple to set up like a WD My Cloud Drive is perfect.

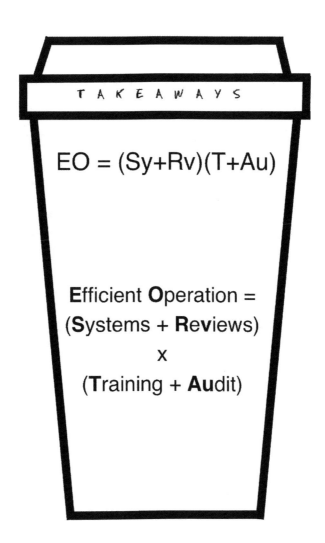

TAKEAWAYS

EO = (Sy+Rv)(T+Au)

Efficient **O**peration =
(**S**ystems + **R**eviews)
x
(**T**raining + **Au**dit)

Financial Controls

The very first thing you need to do is to find a great accountant. They should be someone who you can relate to and will be able to talk to you straight. Someone local with experience in the restaurant business would be a good starting point. Ask for recommendations from other businesses and then arrange an interview with them. Make sure that they are accessible if you need advice and that you will be able to speak to them directly.

We chose our accountant following a recommendation and an interview. We have been very thankful for the advice and clear perspective he and his team have always given us. When we have been at difficult points in our journey, they have been available at short notice to crunch the numbers, put things in easy to understand formats and allowed us to get the best result we could in negotiations. They have also made sure that our company legal obligations are met, as well as help train us on using the accounts package to maintain day to day operations.

Setting up the type of company you want to trade from is critical and you must take professional advice, but our guess is that for any coffee shop you would need to be set up as a Limited Company and be registered for VAT. It is unlikely that any coffee business that takes less than the threshold for VAT would be profitable anyway.

There are a few ways to manage your accounting. Let the accountant do everything, you do some of it yourself and then get your accountant to validate and do year-end, or you employ a bookkeeper to help. You need to weigh up the cost versus your time equation here. Doing some of the day-to-day invoice management will help you stay very focused on the business.

You will need to choose an accounting package. We chose Sage as our accountant recommended it and worked with it. Today there are many to choose from but we still advise you to speak to your accountant before making the final decision.

Agree with your accountant exactly what they will do for you, how much you will do yourself and what you need to provide, to allow them to do their job efficiently for you.

The coffee shop business model.

A coffee shop is an attractive business because of the high profits of the products it sells and the relatively low start up costs. However the fixed costs of operating such as rent and rates, and the variable costs such as staffing and power, can mean that the level of sales needed to breakeven is high. Therefore understanding your breakeven sales figure is a key element of success, as once the breakeven is achieved, then sales above this level produce about a 50% profit.

There is a breakeven calculator spreadsheet available to download at www.dailygrindbook.com/resources

The capacity of the business to take money is a limiting factor as coffee shop trade is not equal across the day or the week with the majority of sales happening in bursts, mostly in the mornings and on the weekends. The maximum customers you can serve per hour with one machine and a well-trained team is about sixty, so that will be your maximum throughput irrespective of the demand. You will find that your guests will not join a queue or line of more than six as well.

Business plan

Having a business plan will help you in many areas of your business. It will help you get funding and get a lease. It will also give you clarity and targets for your whole team. Remember without a plan you won't know how you are doing. When the business starts up you will be very busy and will need to make time to constantly review your progress.

There are thousands of books written on putting together business plans. We have used Live Plan, an online business-planning tool that takes you through every part of putting a business plan together.

Borrowing money and dealing with banks

You may need to borrow money to start your business, or you may want to. It depends on your circumstances. Even if you have enough saved to start a business, your accountant may recommend you borrow as well, to start a relationship with a bank or because of tax efficiency. There are now many more ways to raise finance than just a bank, such as with crowd funding etc.

Banks are mostly interested in how you will be able to pay back the loan and what happens if the business is not successful. They will want to mitigate their risks in a number of ways; they may want a personal guarantee in the form of a charge on your house or other assets or from another person willing to back you.

The bank manager of old, where decisions were made at a local level is no more. Your bank manager will be responsible for correctly completing the paperwork that will allow head office to make the final decision. This is not to say that a good bank manager is not an asset. In our experience ours has given us great advice and guided us through the maze as well as giving us a reality check when needed.

So keeping them in the loop, managing your cash flow well and preventing any surprises, is the key to a good relationship.

Coffee shops are cash businesses, where the guest pays on receipt of the goods so should always operate with a cash surplus in their accounts. However, there are predictable and unpredictable demands on that cash, which may flatter the bank balance, so managing your cash flow is critical.

Cash flow

Working out your cash flow for the next six months or a year is very important too. Our businesses tend to have peaks and troughs in trade combined with quarterly obligations to HMRC and rent. So your bank balance won't tell you anything about the health of your business.

Our cash flow forecaster has saved us from problems countless times. It's simpler than it sounds and although there are some online systems you can use, we have set up a simple spreadsheet. We estimate sales and costs weekly going forward which provides us with a projected end of week cash balance in our bank.

If you forecast a cash flow shortfall in plenty of time, suppliers would rather you be upfront and honest rather than burying your head in the sand and ignoring it.

We have an example of our cash flow forecaster to download at www.dailygrindbook.com/resources

Payroll

You will need to decide whether to run payroll internally or through an outside supplier. Decide whether your payroll will run weekly, fortnightly or monthly. Look at the impact on your cash flow and your employees. Paying monthly will be the simplest and easiest and although paying in cash will reduce your bank charges, paying directly into their bank account is probably the best solution for security and compliance.

Out of all the things we did, we found payroll one of the most complicated. You can do it online at the HMRC website or on another third party platform such as Sage. Either way it's very important to get your teams wages right, for moral reasons, keeping them happy, as well as the legal obligations to HMRC.

The added complexity of auto enrolment for pensions will add another cost to your business. Choose your company pensions advisor carefully. Once you have chosen your pension provider, you will need to decide whether to manually calculate and administer payments, or use a payroll system which will make the process easier and less time consuming but will add cost.

Whether you outsource or do internal payroll, it is essential that each week the manager must ensure your team are paid correctly. We use a payroll tracker, which is a spreadsheet where the manager inserts the hours worked each day into the tracker. This tracker shows the manager how much has been spent on wages, so that he doesn't go over the agreed budget. As well as this we have a signing in and out sheet that the team member completes themselves as a record of their attendance. An example of this payroll tracking spreadsheet can be downloaded from www.dailygrindbook.com/resources

Budget

Having a budget for everything, including your sales and costs is essential. In the early days just do a best guess budget and then review it and try and better it. Here are some key budget percentages you should aim for:

- Cost of goods < 25%
- Payroll cost < 30%
- Rents and rates < 10%
- Utilities < 10%
- Other costs < 10%

Team cost

When calculating team costs, you need to include the employers National Insurance and the company pension contribution. There is a hidden cost when taking on new team members as we have already discussed, the cost of lost productivity. So you will need to build this into your budget at the start of the business and expect the team cost to be higher at the start.

Product mix

When you know the theoretical profit on everything, you can put that data into your till system which will give you a weekly report. Adding this information to the till is something many people don't bother with. Your till system will be able to provide you with so much data, that will help you make the right decisions on range and pricing simply and easily.

Recipes

Adding an extra slice of bacon or cheese in a sandwich can move your profit down considerably and unless everything has a recipe card that is followed this will happen. Using photographs in the recipe cards will help your team present consistent products.

Waste

When looking at the profitability of products, make sure you include any waste incurred. There is no reason to stock products with a high profit if they don't sell and have to be put in the bin.

Stock taking

You will need to do regular stocktaking for the following reasons:

- You can work out your real profit and keep it on track.
- You will carry less stock, as you will know exactly what you have. Therefore you will have more money in your bank account and not in your suppliers' bank accounts.
- Your storeroom will be tidier and you will save time looking for items.
- You will have less theft, as the team will know you are checking regularly.

You should do it at least every month but ideally every week. You don't need to do it yourself either but have a simple way of counting and calculating the stock level.

We just use an order form spreadsheet with an extra column to add the total value of the stock counted.

Once we started doing stocktaking regularly, things got better in a number of areas. The amount of stock we were carrying reduced, which reduced waste through easier rotation of stock. Also it was easier to order what you needed as everyone could see what we had. Our gross profit went up by about 3% as there was less waste, fewer damages and the temptation to steal was reduced as any stock that was taken would be missed straight away. Importantly, our money stayed in our bank for longer.

Weekly profit calculations

Another important reason to take stock weekly, is to be able to work out how much money you are making week by week, rather than wait for the month end accounts to be done.

Having a basic understanding of what you spend and what you take, and what you are left with at the end of the week, will give you a good idea if you are on track to make money.

When you are doing your budgeting you should calculate a minimum breakeven sales figure for each week and then each day.

You can use the numbers from this breakeven calculation to set up a simple spreadsheet that you can use weekly to estimate your weekly profit. It may not be exactly accurate to the penny but will alert you to any impending problems.

You can find an example of a simple profit tracker at www.dailygrindbook.com/resources

A wise café owner once said to me 'everyone that works for you is taking their bus fare home, the problem occurs when that start taking their taxi fare'. In other words everyone will be taking something from you so by taking stock and calculating your profit weekly you will at least be able to keep a close eye on this.

In their book, 'Setting up and managing your own coffee bar', Hugh and John (Gilmartin & Richardson) tell the story of the man in the brown suit. When he was asked to invest in their business, he asked them a simple question that they couldn't answer. 'How much money did you make last week?'

He told them, 'I record what I buy every day and record my sales every day. At the end of the week I count up all the wages and recount the stock…..I have my profit. I just take off the rent and a few other things and I have my profit. Every week. Every single week. I count at the start, count at the end and record during the week. Now is that hard?'

It's not complicated; you must know your profit every week.

Involve your team

Ask a member of your team how much money the coffee shop makes and they will normally guess at between 30% and 50% of the sales versus the actual of between 5% and 15%. All they see is the cash going into the till and do a mental calculation of what they think you make. Share with them the costs they don't see, put up utility bills on the wall, and take electricity readings weekly and let them know the real level of profit is far less than they think.

Build in refit costs in three years time

Whatever money you make at the end of the year you need to consider the cost of refurbishing the guest areas and replacing equipment.

Lots of businesses come unstuck here and don't keep their business looking fresh leading to guests moving away to the latest shiny business to open close by.

VAT

Don't forget the VAT. Most things you sell will be subject to VAT and as we have already said, it's unlikely that you will not be a VAT registered business. You will become a tax collector and every three months send a good chunk of money to HMRC. It's likely that the first couple of VAT returns will be low, as you will be claiming back the cost of the equipment you bought for the set up, so you may even get a refund from HMRC. This is again where your cash flow forecasting comes into its own.

As a rule anything that you sell for consumption on the premises is vat-able and a few things that you sell for take away that are not hot will be non vat-able. It's very important to take professional advise on this as the VAT rules are complicated and a little confusing in some areas. When you get a VAT inspection you may be liable for a fine and repaying of the VAT you didn't charge if you get this wrong.

We have known coffee shops go under because of this.

Taking payments

Taking payments can add up to a considerable cost to your business, as banks hate cash and will charge you to deposit it and card processing companies charge you for the pleasure of accepting cards.

Taking cash is by far the cheapest option, costing around 0.6% of the value of the money banked. Of course you need to include in the team cost, the time it takes to count the money and take it to the bank.

The cost to you of taking a card transaction is nowhere near simple to calculate. Debit cards are generally charged at a flat rate of around 20p per transaction and about 10p per transaction for a contactless card. Credit card costs vary, based on the type of card that is used and a percentage of the total transaction which is normally somewhere between 1% and 3% is charged.

So when you accept a credit card, it is virtually impossible to know exactly how much that transaction will cost. We can't think of another business transaction where the real cost is virtually impossible to calculate. Also the money taken by card does not reach your bank account for between three and five days.

You will also need to hire a terminal at around £5-£20 per month, and be Payment Card Industry Data Security Standard (PCI DSS) compliant at an annual cost of about £50.

The key impact on a small business is that the majority of cards taken are debit credit cards.

The following table illustrates a typical cost of taking each of the different types of cards versus cash.

	Fee/cost to retailer for a £3 transaction	% Of transaction
Cash	1.8p	0.6%
Debit Card	20p	6.7%
Contactless Card	10p	3.3%
Credit Card	6p	2%

You can reduce banking charges in a few ways. Open a bank account that has no cash deposit fees such as with the post office and offer cash back at the till with debit card transactions.

Do your homework; don't just accept your banks preferred card handler. Get a few to give a quote and look into the scheme's offered by the Federation of Small Businesses (FSB) and Bookers.

Till processes

You need to have a solid till process that needs to cover the following:

- Refund policy - all refunds need to be recorded and double signed with the reason for the refund clearly stated. This will allow you to look for trends over time as well; if you are having refunds on the same product over a few weeks then it could be an issue with the recipe or storage of that product that you will need to address.

- Discount policy - local businesses, student, loyalty cards, and good will. Put some thought into all these things.

- Forged notes training – we have found having a UV detector near the till deters criminals from trying to get you to accept forged notes and makes it easy for the team to spot forgeries.

- Cash up process - whether on the till or on a separate spreadsheet.

- A process to manage change ordering from the bank - remember banks charge to deposit cash and to get change.

- A petty cash routine – you will need to buy some things locally in an emergency and if you lose the receipt then you lose the money.

- Rules around how often the banking happens – we bank every day and get a stamp in the paying in book as proof. This has been very valuable over time as banks do make mistakes and without a stamp it's difficult to prove. We never use the fast drop, as you don't get a receipt. It is often not counted in branch but sent to a cash centre and sometimes didn't get credited to our account for days.

- A weekly/daily management check process – if you don't do the cashing up yourself every day then you will need to have a set of checks to ensure there are no mistakes.

- Review of till audit reports - pull off a few operator audit reports and you can compare the performance of the team against each other for things like voiding or cancelling the last item, no sales, refunds etc.

- Credit card reconciliation – the credit and debit cards will be deposited into your account after a few days. Check every deposit to ensure it matches, as mistakes happen here as well.

- Check the correct amount is deposited into the bank every day - use online banking and if a deposit isn't seen, check that your team have put it in.

- Empty the till drawer at night - leave the drawer open so that anyone can see there is no money in it. If someone does break in they won't break the till drawer trying to steal the cash!

- Serving friends and family policy - something like the following policy.

Team Food Rules & Discount Policy

- The daily allowance for team food, is to allow you to have a meal for your break, while you are in work.
- It is only for food to be eaten while in work, and not as an allowance to buy stock to take home later or to be passed on to another person or guest.
- It must be recorded in the correct way on the till and the receipt signed by a colleague.
- While you are working you are also allowed to have free tea and coffee for your personal consumption.

- When not working and as a guest you are entitled to a 10% discount for your own personal consumption on drinks and food, excluding merchandise.

Company/organisational/voucher discounts

- Some local businesses and organisations as well as students and members of the armed forces are entitled to a 10% discount that must be recorded on the till; this list will be specific per store.
- Only one voucher can be used per transaction.
- Only one type of discount can be used per transaction, either a stamped loyalty card OR a bus key card or student discount.
- Some vouchers do not need to be printed and can be shown on a phone e.g. O2 moments, Foursquare, Facebook, or email discounts. You must record the code or deal on the receipt.

Free coffee card stamp

- Every stamp is worth money so should be given only for drinks purchased that are on the menu board.
- A pre stamped card can only be give to a guest following a complaint or a problem with their order, to encourage the guest to come back again.

Serving family or close friends

- Ideally you should not serve family or close friends on the till. You should always ask someone to take over the till for that transaction. Occasionally this will be difficult so make a colleague aware of the fact.
- *The control of discounts and deals is very important to the business, to ensure that guests and team are not embarrassed or compromised. If you are uncertain about anything then please talk to your manager.*
- *Abuse of team food allowance and giving or taking of any unauthorised discounts will be treated as Gross Misconduct under the company's disciplinary procedure.*

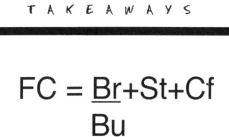

T A K E A W A Y S

$$FC = \frac{Br + St + Cf}{Bu}$$

Financial Control =
Breakeven / **Bu**dgets +
Stocktaking + **C**ashflow

Marketing Your Coffee Shop

The four P's: Product, Place, Price and Promotion.

Whenever you read a book on marketing they will talk about the four P's. What you sell, the **Product**, where you sell it, the **Place**, what you sell it for, the **Price** and how you tell people about what you sell i.e. advertising, the **Promotion**.

In practice it's easier to think of the three M's, **Market, Message, Media** and they need to be done in that order.

Most entrepreneurs start with the message, i.e. what's great about their coffee shop and why you should visit, without considering the needs of the market or the people who are going to be buying from you.

You should always start with the market. Who is going to be your guest, what are their needs, desires and what problem have they got that you can help with?

It's a really good idea to work out who your top five types of guests will be and give them a name. Then you will be able to target your message directly to them.

Here is an example of a template we use to do this; you can download a copy from www.dailygrindbook.com/resources

GUEST AVATAR	Name
How old are they?	
Male or female?	
What is the purpose of their visit?	
What's their favourite drink and food?	
How do they dress?	
Who do they visit with?	
What time do they visit?	
What do they worry about? Diet, health, value, variety, service, quality	
What are their needs?	
What can we do to make them Raving Fans or what would attract them to visit more often?	

Once you know who your guest is, you can craft a Message that will be of interest to them. It's a good idea to have the avatar document in front of you when you are putting together any marketing.

Then you can think of where to advertise and what media to use, but remember the marketing of your coffee shop is a combination of everything you do everywhere.

We have put together a load of ideas later in the book about marketing for no or little money.

Understanding the value of each guest and how much to spend to get a new one!

Before you spend a penny on marketing, you need to work out how much each guest is worth to you. Not just by what they spend each day but what they are likely to spend over their lifetime as a guest. For example, if a guest spends on average £5 a visit and visits you once a week for 52 weeks of the year and stays with you for 5 years before they move away or die, then their value to you is $5 \times 52 \times 5 = £1300$. Or if they are more regular and come in 5 days a week and spend £5 per day and stay for 5 years, they would be worth $5 \times 5 \times 52 \times 5 = £6500$.

This is a useful calculation to explain to your team how important each individual guest is to the business. It is very easy for your team to get blasé when dealing with the same guest who spends a small amount every day and starts to get on their nerves. This can be very dangerous, so when you explain to your team that the value of each guest is not just the amount they spend per day, it's the amount they spend over the lifetime of being your guest, it can make a difference to the way they treat people. We like to compare a salesman who is selling a £6000 piece of furniture to a guest. Ask your team to put themselves in that salesman's shoes and then ask them a question. How would you treat that guest who was going to spend £6000 with you? The answer is inevitably 'like royalty' or 'I would roll out the red carpet.'

When dealing with difficult guests, we ask our team to imagine the guest has £6000 tattooed on their forehead. This helps the team put the importance of dealing with the complaint or grizzly guest into perspective and hopefully will make them take the right decision and adopt the right attitude when dealing with them, to ensure they continue to be guests. As we all know a guest who is treated well when they have a complaint or issue will become one of our most loyal guests, as well as telling their friends how good we are.

Your colours and logo

You will need to come up with a logo and when you do that you will need to consider your colour palette.

There are some great online resources for this and this site is one of the best ones https://www.slalom.com/thinking/visual-analytics-101-the-art-and-science-of-color (Slalom).

- Black = sophistication, power, mystery, formality, evil, death
- Grey = neutrality, stability, maturity, security, authority, strength
- White = purity, cleanliness, modernity, goodness, hope, freshness
- Brown = natural, dirty/earthy, authentic, richness, simplicity, tradition
- Red = danger, alertness, anger, romance, excitement, energy
- Yellow = caution, energy, cheerful, friendliness, intellect, cowardice
- Green = life, growth, nature, money, envy, sickness
- Blue = peace, stability, calm, tranquillity, integrity, sadness
- Purple = royalty, luxury, passion, magic, wisdom, extravagance
- Pink = romance, compassion, beauty, love, sensitivity, femininity

Internal marketing

Labels

The price label is your most valuable marketing tool. People will not buy unless there is a clear price, as they don't want a shock when they go to the till to pay and get embarrassed. They also want to know what ingredients are in the product for practical purposes. You have a great opportunity to upsell and add value to what you are selling by the description on the label and by using the right words.

There is a whole science devoted to pricing and labelling but here are a few pointers and if you want a great article on this then go to Nick Kolenda (Kolenda):

http://www.nickkolenda.com/psychological-pricing-strategies/

Charm pricing

Changing the left most digits to appear cheaper i.e. 3.00 to 2.99, as the change from 3 to 2 is the most visible difference.

Fluency pricing

A more complicated number is harder to process therefore disagreeable. Fluent pricing is good for emotionally charged prices.

Syllable pricing

A price that has fewer syllables is more agreeable than with multiple syllables. For example, eight pounds fifty seven sound more expensive than nine pounds.

Font choices

Smaller font sizes and less space between letters make a price appear cheaper.

Anchor numbers

Anchor numbers are numbers displayed before prices to generate a subconscious comparison between that number and your prices. E.g. If your coffee shop or café has a 4 in its branding and is displayed everywhere, then the guest has a natural attraction to the number 4 (4, 14, 40,400) that means they are more prepared to agree with it as a price.

Decoy product

A decoy product is used to compare products and rationalize a consumer to go for the product you want them to. See the following example.

- **Web Only**: £59
- **Print Only**: £125
- **Web and Print**: £125

When this was tested, no one purchased the print only product as it is a terrible product with terrible cost and purchased the products the company wanted them to buy i.e. the web only product.

No currency signs

By having no currency signs, you remove the monetary value of the items a little bit, taking away the fear of purchasing.

Time related advertising

If the product is associated with time, it typically trends better than stating cost or just enjoyment.

I.e. saying 'spend some TIME enjoying our coffee' works better than 'enjoy our coffee', the reason being, that consumers connect better with paying for time with a product rather than taking the product.

Justify discounts

By justifying discount prices to the consumer in a way that is either relatable or perceived as a reward to them, makes them much more prepared to purchase that discounted product. Don't allow negative assumptions to creep in to the weave of their thoughts on the product.

Use small price increments instead of large price changes

By making small price increases frequently over a long period of time, people will not see the overall price increase nor will they feel cheated.

Decrease product sizes

Instead of increasing price, we can decrease product volume. Again this must be approached with caution however as this tactic can lead to mistrust from regular guests.

Your Website

When you are designing your website you should think about what its real purpose is, and how it integrates with your marketing plan.

Your website will be used by your guests to:

- Check your opening hours
- Check your menu
- Get your telephone number
- Send you a message

Your objectives when people visit your website are to:

- Get their contact details

- Get them to like or follow you on social media
- Answer any objections in their mind as to why they would not visit you
- Use a Facebook pixel to build a custom audience in Facebook for remarketing

Getting your website visitors to connect with you in some form or another will allow you to continue to communicate with them. Either through getting them signed up to your loyalty or VIP club by filling in a sign up form or by following you on social media.

You must have a Google analytics code and a Facebook tracking pixel included in the website. This will allow you to see how many visitors you are getting and how they found your website as well as building a Facebook audience that you can market to.

Your website must be mobile device friendly and display responsively on different sizes of screens. Most modern websites will do this automatically, but check that this is the case as websites that don't will not show up on Google searched on a mobile device.

We have talked earlier about the importance of a loyalty/VIP club and how it will help you communicate to your customers directly. A sign up form on your website will be an important method of getting new members.

To get your website to appear on page one of Google for a search for coffee shops in your area is key. To stand a better chance of achieving this you need to ensure; that your business details are exactly the same on every social media and listing website that you join, you register a Google + page for your business, your website includes key words that people will be searching for including the location. When you get reviews on TripAdvisor they will feature on Google's results too so take control of your own TripAdvisor page.

Stamped loyalty cards

The traditional way coffee shops have encouraged repeat purchasing has been through the use of the stamped loyalty card. This is an effective and simple way of getting guests to become regular visitors. Many people carry multiple cards so getting yours to stand out is vital. So think about the design and how you word the offer on the card. A pre-stamped tenth coffee free is more attractive than a card with nine empty stamps on it.

Joint ventures

This is where you team up with local non-competing businesses to offer a deal to their customers. They work well when a business or organisation has a wait time built in. Here is a selection of joint ventures that we have used:

- Local theatre - discount for theatre goers on their website
- Bus tours - free water or buy one get one free, on showing their ticket, making sure it is printed on the ticket for us
- O2 priority moments - free to join for small businesses, sending vouchers to local O2 guests on their phone
- Local town loyalty card - access to the mailing list of all holders
- Travel agents - they give away our vouchers
- Language schools
- Art week partner - using our facilities as a place to display their work for the duration of the art week. Also as a venue to launch the week off
- Folk week partner - as a venue for artists included in the programme
- Network meetings - after close
- Runners and cycling groups - meet before and after the run (with cycling groups its often a good idea to think about being a halfway stop off so the cycle club could be ten or twenty miles away)
- Dry cleaners
- Taxi drivers

- Hairdressers
- Music clubs
- Games clubs
- Gyms
- Car garages
- Estate agents

Business accounts

We have had a lot of success with local business accounts. If we find a local business using us regularly, we will offer them a business account, sometimes with a discount. This means that they pay us monthly for their food and drinks, which we record separately. The benefit to them is that they don't need to process lots of receipts and they can put it through their books in a very tax efficient way.

Support local causes

Be generous when a local charity, school, hospital, society etc. asks you for support. Only provide them with a product or a voucher for a product, not cash as this will have a double benefit of bringing people to your establishment, as well as generating goodwill with all those at the event. We made a 'Bank of Java&Co' voucher, which we use to give away to good causes. We have a rule that they should be very local to us as we get many requests from charities that have no local presence.

Suspended coffee scheme

This is a perfect way to support a local cause. The idea comes from Italy where the well off in the village would buy an extra cup of coffee for someone less fortunate to collect later. We were one of the first in the UK to do a suspended coffee scheme but we adapted the idea to ensure it was fairer for everyone. When a guest buys a suspended coffee from us, 100% of the cost goes to our chosen charity, The Gatehouse in Oxford, rather than us just providing a coffee and taking a profit off the sale. This works brilliantly and so far we have raised over £3000.

It's given us a real Unique Selling Point (USP) and a good feeling for both our guests and us.

Oxford Mail 22nd April 2013 (Oxford Mail, 2013):

Pair's web coffee fad a 'perc' for homeless

By Katriona Ormiston, Reporter   6:00pm Monday 22nd April 2013 in News
covering West Oxford, Botley and the Vale of White Horse. Call me on (01865) 425426

HOT IDEA: From left, Megan Greet, Andrew Smith, project director at Gatehouse, and Claire and Andrew Bowen

Buy this photo »

COFFEE shop owners Andrew and Claire Bowen were stirred into helping the city's homeless after stumbling across a Facebook phenomenon.

The couple, who run Java & Co shops in Abingdon and Oxford, perked up when they saw how Suspended Coffee – which encourages people to buy a second cup for someone in need – was turning into a global trend on the social networking site.

Mr Bowen, 49, said: "It was just something I came across on Facebook and thought 'blooming hell', that's a good idea."

Anyone ordering a coffee from their shops in New Inn Hall Street, Oxford, and Market Place, Abingdon, can also pay £1.50 to be donated to homeless shelter The Gatehouse in St Giles.

Mr Bowen said: "It has gone all across the world, so we wanted to bring it to Oxfordshire.

"We are a local coffee shop and we wanted to keep it local and support the homeless in Oxford and make a positive impact.

"We have only just launched and it is already proving pretty popular.

Oxford Mail 29th May 2014 (Oxford Mail, 2014):

CHARITY AID: Cafe scheme brings in badly needed funds for work

Extra cups of coffee add up
to a big boost for homeless

Rachel Bayne

rbayne@oxfordmail.co.uk

COFFEE lovers and tea drinkers have raised more than £1,000 for a homeless charity by adding a second cup to their bill for someone in need.

Customers of Oxford's Java&Co have bought 550 "suspended" coffees" in the last year and the funds raised have to gone to the Gatehouse.

The scheme – the first of its kind in the city – started when owners Andrew and Claire Bowen were stirred into action by a post on Facebook.

Mr Bowen, 50, said: "I had a customer contact us on Facebook. We looked it up and realised it was a global movement which started in Italy and has gone viral. But we had never heard of it. I thought it was a really good idea.

"We're really pleased with how well it is doing and the fact that it is still growing. Our hope is that other cafes and other restaurants in Oxford will set up a scheme of their own."

A year after its adoption, the coffee shop has raised £1,300 through customers spending an extra £1.50 for a suspended coffee.

The owners said some regular customers come in each week just to buy a suspended coffee.

The coffee shop in New Inn Hall Street has hosted other charity events throughout the year such as auctioning paintings to help raise funds.

HAPPY TO HELP: Andrew and Claire Bowen at Java & Co, which raises money for the homeless   Picture: OM/14876 Mark Hemsworth

Mrs Bowen, 50, said: "We are absolutely delighted that it has been so successful and the total that has been received has been phenomenal.

"We are so pleased that our customers are supporting such a good cause and we've always encouraged it to go further."

The Gatehouse opens for two hours each evening and is a drop-in centre for the homeless.

Andrew Smith, from the charity based at the St Giles parish rooms in Woodstock Road, said: "I was amazed to hear from the Javaistas that some customers come in specially just to buy a suspended coffee because they know that the money will go directly to

support our work. Homeless people really appreciate the help they receive from local business. It makes them feel part of the community."

Jaxson Marc Frater, 44, lived on the streets for 26 years before he started volunteering for the charity.

He said: "It means so much to the Gatehouse. It keeps us ticking over and we are able to expand and get names for the guests to enjoy.

"The Gatehouse has helped me over the past 13 or 14 years. I did appreciate it and that is why I wanted to give something back.

"I had the opportunity and I took it with both hands."

The suspended coffee scheme originated in Italy before becoming a global phenomenon on Facebook last year.

It is said to have originated more than 100 years ago in working-class cafes in Naples, Italy.

When someone experienced good luck they would buy a second coffee to be put aside.

Those in need would then approach cafes to ask if any of the pre-paid coffees were available.

WHERE THE MONEY GOES

▲ **CUSTOMERS** can donate £1.50 to the Gatehouse at Java&Co. Ask for a suspended coffee at the counter, and £1.50 will be put into a collection tin for the charity.

The whole amount then goes to the Gatehouse, at the St Giles parish rooms in Woodstock Road, where homeless people can get a cuppa six days a week. There are

on average 50 to 55 guests for each session.

According to figures from Oxford Homeless Pathways, around 56 homeless people aged 22 and over use emergency accommodation at Oxford's O'Hanlon House and the city is also estimated to have one of the highest numbers of people sleeping rough in the UK.

Marketing automation

You can communicate directly to your guests using an email-marketing platform such as Mail Chimp or Get Response.

We have had a lot of success with our VIP Scheme. In summary, when people join our VIP Scheme they get a free drink for joining as an incentive to join. Then they will get a series of pre written emails over the next few months that will be a mixture of offers and information about why we are different, what we stand for and the products we sell. When we have a new product or seasonal event, or something happening locally we will also send out an email informing them. On their birthday they will get a voucher for a free piece of cake to celebrate. Then seven days after their birthday they get an email asking them if they had a good birthday and enjoyed the cake and to please give us a quick review on either Facebook or TripAdvisor.

We have found that it has been a very cost effective way of building our business and keeping us in the front of mind for guests. All the offers we send out are profitable and get guests to try things that they may not ever have tried. It has allowed us to build a relationship with our guests quicker and has also been a great way of getting feedback through surveys.

We collect guest's details at the till, on our website, using competitions and through joint ventures with other organisations.

More details of this and training on how to set a similar scheme for your coffee shop is available at:

www.cafesuccesshub.com/vipclub

Getting PR coverage

Getting coverage in your local newspaper or radio stations can be easier than you think. Journalists are always looking for new stories, particularly from people like you, local Independent businesses that are relevant to their audience.

You just need to think like a journalist and prepare a story for them. Think about why the story is interesting and worth publishing.

Simple things often work well like:

- Anniversaries – your coffee shop has been open for x years
- National days – you are taking part in/ have taken part in national coffee/vegetarian/cake week or day
- Surveys – commenting on a survey that is relevant to you
- Awards
- Trends

- Charity involvement

We have included examples of coverage we have had with the press and the press release for our Suspended Coffee Scheme. We have also been interviewed numerous times on the local radio stations.

Oxford Mail 1st October 2014 (Oxford Mail, 2014):

Coffee day stirs up interest

Ash Fielder, 28, owner Andrew Bowen, 49, and Maria Kourou, 24, with a hill of beans

Wednesday 1 October 2014 / News

Share

Want more local stories like these, direct to your inbox?   Enter your email address   **Sign up**

COFFEE shops across the city embraced International Coffee Day, a celebration of the much-loved beverage, with the focus very much on Fairtrade.

Staff at Java & Co in George Street were among those to spread the message to their customers on Monday.

Owner Andrew Bowen said: "The whole purpose of the day was to raise awareness that farmers should get a fair price for their coffee."

In February the Oxford celebrated its 10th anniversary of becoming a Fairtrade city. Sebastian Blake, chairman of Oxfordshire Fairtrade Coaltion, said: "All moves to promote fairtrade globally are welcome, Oxford has always been a leader in this area."

FOR IMMEDIATE RELEASE

Co⬛⬛
Tel: ⬛⬛
em⬛⬛⬛⬛⬛⬛uk

SUSPENDED COFFEE COMES TO OXFORD & ABINGDON

Java&Co Oxford & Abingdon Launch 'Suspended Coffee' to support The Gatehouse a local charity for the homeless and poorly housed in St Giles Oxford

On the 19th April 2013 Andrew and Claire Bowen the owners of Java&Co Oxford and Abingdon are joining the global movement of 'Suspended Coffee' to support The Gatehouse in Oxford.

The idea for a suspended coffee originates from Italy. Traditionally where someone has experienced good luck they buy 2 coffees but consume only one and the other goes to someone who cant afford to buy their own. Its called a Caffe Sospeso.

It's a random act of kindness that Andrew and Claire loved so much, they have adapted the idea to work by partnering with The Gatehouse. From Friday 19th April, customers at Java&Co in Oxford or Abingdon will be able to add a suspended coffee for £1.50 to their order and 100% of that will be passed on to The Gatehouse, a charity for the homeless and poorly housed in St Giles Oxford.

Andrew explained 'We had a Facebook message from a customer telling us about Suspended Coffee 3 weeks ago and we immediately thought of the Gatehouse in Oxford, as they were near neighbours until they moved to St Giles. When we discussed the idea with them we thought it be fairer to give them the donations rather than the coffee, which will benefit all of their visitors.

Andrew Smith from The Gatehouse explained. 'When Java&Co approached us we were delighted, it seemed such a simple idea and it is great that all the money raised will stay local in the heart of the city. We have an increasing number of people who rely on us whether its for food, warmth or just company. We are open 6 days a week'

The hope is that other Coffee Shops and Restaurants in Oxford will come on board. A Facebook and Twitter account have been set up to promote the idea, join in the conversation at www.facebook.com/SuspendedCoffeeOxfordshire and @CaffesospesoOX.

We are happy to do photos and interviews to explain more about the scheme.
ENDS
Notes to Editor
Java&Co is a Local Independent Coffee Shop with branches on New Inn Hall St Oxford and Market Place Abingdon www.javaandco.co.uk
The Gatehouse is an Oxford Charity based in St Giles Oxford supporting about 50 Homeless or badly housed people with food, clothing and other essentials. www.oxfordgatehouse.org/#
Wikipedia http://en.wikipedia.org/wiki/Caffe_sospeso

On your press release you need the following things:

- Contact details

- A catchy headline

- A first paragraph summary of the story

- The detail of the story

- A few quotes from you or others involved

- A summary of what your business is

- Other sources that may be useful to the journalist

Deadlines

- With newspapers you need to be working a couple of weeks in advance of publication.

- With magazines you need to be working at least 6 weeks in advance of publication.

- With radio and TV they can turn press releases around within 24 hours, but do give them advance notice of something big.

- Typically newspaper deadlines are mid-day Tuesday for publication on Thursday. Ideally they should have received your press release by Monday to give you a chance of inclusion the same week.

Send it in the body of an email as well as an attachment as the journalist may want to copy and paste some of the text and sometimes they don't open attachments.

A template for a doing a press release is available to download at: www.dailygrindbook.com/resources

Newspaper/magazine/radio/brochure advertising

We have rarely found these to work effectively, they are expensive and it's very difficult to calculate a return on investment. The very nature of these forms of media are that they cover a large area and unless you are a destination on your own e.g. in a garden centre, then the people you advertise to are unlikely to make a special trip to your coffee shop.

One thing we have had great success with here with is advertorials in local newspapers, where we give something away to their readers, in exchange for an article in the newspaper.

Our most successful promotion was when we gave away a free sandwich to every reader of our local paper. It cost us £280 of ingredients and we gave away 400 sandwiches but many people bought a coffee at the same time as well. We had a full coffee shop on the day, and lots of new guests forever. Everyone was happy, the newspaper were delighted as they printed and sold many more copies that day and had people out selling them on the high street as well.

We could not have got that sort of return on investment from a standard advert anywhere else.

Social media

An amazing fact is – one in five activities on the Internet is now for Facebook.

Most business owners are aware how important social media can be for their business and they think that it's easy to do. Lots of these people have tried and got nowhere and a few just can't even be bothered.

If you think that social media is the way to fill up your coffee shop with eager guests, then you need to understand how it all works and treat it like you would anything else you want to be a success.

We had a chat with a fellow coffee shop owner, about what we both do for marketing and he told us, 'I can't be bothered with Facebook and all that!'

When we explained that if he doesn't, his guests would anyway his jaw dropped. He didn't realise that every coffee shop and café now has a social media presence, whether the business owners like it or not!

When we showed him what was online in these networks about his business, he needed a chill pill! Not because it was all bad but because he realised that he was missing a great way to build a relationship with his guests and to deal with any issues quickly and turn any negatives into positives.

Even if you are not on Facebook, then a page could have been generated automatically for you or put there by a guest. You don't need to be on Twitter, Foursquare, Pinterest, Instagram, Snapchat or TripAdvisor or half a dozen others to be complemented or complained about!

As they say, you need to be 'In it to win it' and you have no option but to get involved.

Finding time was a big concern for him, as there are only 24hrs in the day. However with a little bit of setting up, the use of a smart phone and delegating some tasks to his team, he could manage it effectively in very little time.

Tools like Hootsuite and the Facebook Pages app are free and great ways to keep up to date and to add content.

There is a trend for everyone to only use social media to communicate. So if they have a question about your business, chances are they will jump onto Facebook or Twitter and send you a message rather than find your email address or phone number to contact you. The number of job enquiries we get that come via Facebook is an example of that.

We read recently about a new way of complaining, via a website that tracks all correspondence with a business and if no satisfactory conclusion for the guest is reached then that business will be exposed on all social media. Although its sounds like it's aimed at big corporations, imagine getting on the wrong side of this and how much damage it could have on your small business.

There is a cumulative effect to all these networks, with the Internet having a very long memory. Everything that has ever been said about your business is searchable online. This will have an impact on your Google rankings and searchability.

What social media doesn't do
Work automatically; you need to treat it like any other thing in your business that you want to succeed, with energy, measures and review.

Give you total control; whenever you engage with a guest on any level it's unpredictable to some extent. So with social media you need to watch the engagement carefully.

Fill up your business overnight with new guests; we would be rich if we had a pound for the number of times we have spoken to new business owners whose marketing plan is 'we'll send out a tweet and then everyone will come running.' Of course there are some high profile companies that have millions of followers where this works but in our experience a tweet may bring in a few extra guests if you are lucky.

It's not for selling on; it's for engaging with people, getting them to know, like and trust you. You are talking to them in their leisure time and people generally aren't receptive to selling then.

What it can do

Get you higher up Google ranking; if you set up all your accounts with the same information in the same way. The address, telephone number and email address should be the same on each platform.

Your guests will find out more about you and become very loyal. By sharing details of your story, your values and your team they will engage with your business at a much greater level.

Complaints and issues can be resolved much quicker by picking them up on social media before they escalate.

Setting up a private Facebook group is a great way to communicate to your teams. From putting up rotas, to arranging meetings and keeping everyone up to date on what is going on.

You can target advertising to people who are interested in what you sell or do. Using a Facebook pixel on your website will allow you to serve ads to people who have visited your website, directly to their Facebook timeline.

It's easy to get testimonials or recommendations to use in your marketing from Facebook or Twitter.

Because of the informality and immediacy of this medium, your guests will give you feed back and questions that they would have previously only talked to their mates about.

The pitfalls

So many business owners using social media link all their accounts together and send out the same message on all social media platforms, completely forgetting about their guests needs. Posting the relevant message for each social media will stop people from turning off your brand.

It will only work if you have a plan

It's like your own Public Relations dept. PR will amplify whatever is going on in your business, good or bad.

You must get the basics right first. Your business must be consistent and working well before you want to advertise it, and it's the same with social media.

You can spend hours on social media with little return.

You need to get the whole team involved for ideas for posts. Having a social media calendar to plan your week is a really good idea.

Clear signage in your coffee shop and on your website, that you are on all these different social media channels is essential and a simple way of getting new followers.

Get your guests details

Ultimately you must get their details so that you are in charge of communicating to them, not the social media giant who can change the rules tomorrow, causing you to lose all contact with your followers or have to pay to communicate to them.

Find out names, email addresses, phone numbers and addresses if you can!

Facebook is constantly changing the way it works but there are some fundamental things you need to do, to get the best out of it.

Facebook set up - you must get right

- Set the page up as a business page, completely separate from your personal profile. If you set the page up and pretend it's a person, then you will very likely get blocked in the future when Facebook find out. You can choose what type of page you want but a local business page is probably the best one to choose if you want people to be able to check in.

- Make sure you have more than one administrator on the account; otherwise if your personal account gets blocked or hacked, you might lose access to the page.

- Enter as many details as you can in the about section. The more information you have here about your location, website, opening hours etc. the better, as it helps with your page being found and shown to people in searches.

- Use great photos of the correct size to make your cover page look great.

- Get your Facebook url; the bit after the www.facebook.com/...... When you set up the page you will be automatically given a page url that will have lots of numbers at the end, so when you share your page the url won't be very descriptive. You must select your own url that will be easy to remember

- Set up the 'call to action' button.

Posting best practice

- Set up some of your team to be editors and they can then post on your behalf.

- You can post immediately or you can programme a post to appear at a later time. Use the drop down arrow on the post button and click schedule. You will be able to preload as many posts as you want to in one go. You can check when your fans are looking at their Facebook page, to discover the best time to schedule a post, by clicking on 'Insights' then 'Posts' to see a chart.

- Video and photos are the best way to get more reach, i.e. shares, likes and views.

- Competitions are great for engagement.

- Offers can be set up on your business page.

- You can also set up an event and invite people.

- Ask people a question in a post to get a reply and therefore more coverage.

- Ask people to share your post.

Advertising on Facebook

- NEVER use the BOOST POST button unless of course you want to waste some money in double quick time! Always use the 'Create Adds' tab.
- Set the audience for your advert correctly. You don't want to be paying to advertise to people who are never likely to visit you. Use the location and demographics settings to fine-tune who gets shown the advert.
- Set the costs tightly and ensure you put an end date into your advert.
- Review the advert after it has been going a few hours.
- Use great pictures to get people's attention.
- Select a great headline that will make people click.
- Put a Facebook tracking pixel on your website, so that you can advertise to those people who visit.

Insights

- Visit the 'Insights Tab' at the top of the page regularly. There is lots of information available to you that will help you with marketing your business.

Google +

Google+ is constantly evolving and something that every business needs to be on as it helps with your position on Google search. Set up your page and again make sure that every detail about your business is identical to everywhere else. I.e. the name, address, postcode, telephone number and contact email address, should be the same across all platforms.

You can set your location in Google + on the map too.

Here are some guidelines of the types of content you should use each social media channel for:

Twitter
- Comment on trending issues
- Look for local events and retweet
- Become a news hub for local events yourself
- Ask people to retweet

Facebook
- Post short videos
- Post team photos
- Give weather related posts
- Share local events
- Ask people to share or comment

YouTube

- Post weekly Vlogs (mini videos)
- Post how to videos
- Add new product videos
- Tag correctly and use the closed captions to generate lots of key words for Google

Instagram

- Product photos
- Location photos
- Local event photos

Pinterest

- Lovely foodie photos
- Local landmarks and events

Summary

Ultimately social media is constantly evolving, with new channels coming out almost weekly, it can be a great tool for the independent business as it allows you to connect with your customers in a personal way that the big chains can't. It's almost free and very cost effective if used well. The key thing to remember is that you must get your guests details so that you can be in charge not Facebook or Twitter. They can change their rules overnight and have gradually reduced the number of your fans they show your posts to. Now less than 6% of your posts are shown to your fans and the more fans you get the percentage reach is even lower.

Use social media to get your customers to love you but don't rely on it as your only source of communication with your guests. Getting email addresses and contact details will give you the power to carry on the conversation with your guests on a personal level.

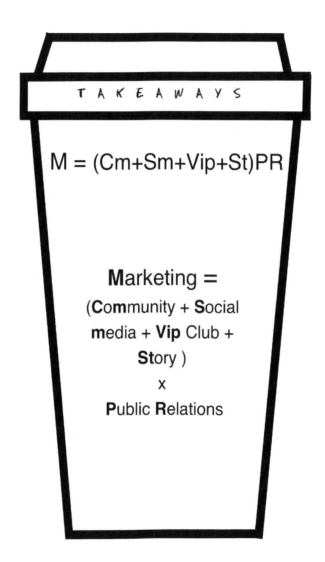

T A K E A W A Y S

M = (Cm+Sm+Vip+St)PR

Marketing =
(**Com**munity + **S**ocial
media + **Vip** Club +
Story)
x
Public **R**elations

When It's Time To Sell

The day may come when you need to sell your business, whether you like it or not. You only need to Google 'coffee shops for sale' to see how many businesses are being offered for much less than their potential value.

The reasons for this are many and varied, but generally there are four underlying causes. The business was set in the wrong location. The owners have had enough, as they have worked six or seven days a week for years. The rent is going up more than they can afford, or there is a shiny new competitor opening close by.

Being able to get a good price for your business is therefore something that needs to be planned for, even before you open the doors on the first day.

A business that runs itself, is systemised and modern will be very attractive to a potential buyer. You need to spend your time working on your coffee shop, not working in it to achieve this.

We looked at the trends in the coffee shop market, and could see the movement towards selling alcohol and offering more food in the evening. We then applied and got restaurant planning permission (A3) and an alcohol licence.

Our business was saleable because we had a profitable business in a great location, a good relationship with our landlord and an established trading history. The fact that we obtained A3 planning and an alcohol licence was a big influence on the value of our business to a prospective buyer.

When we sold one of our coffee shops, it came as a major shock to lots of people who asked us 'why would you sell it?' The answer is that we were made an offer we couldn't refuse and that every business is really up for sale all the time. If anyone tells you differently don't believe them.

So many people we have spoken to have never ever considered an exit plan and so when the time comes to retire or move away, they are not at all prepared. They often get very little reward for all the years of blood, sweat and tears they have put into their business. Even worse, the closure sometimes costs them money.

In our chapter, The Clever Coffee Shop Location, we talked about how important it was to consider the resale value of your coffee shop before even embarking on a site. We truly believe this should be at the forefront of your mind at all times.

The correct advice is essential as you plan in your business. We sought advice from a hospitality expert, who became our 'third brain'. He introduced us to other experts who supported us in positioning the business, to achieve the best return on our investment.

When you sell your business, your team are part of that. We felt strongly that everyone in the team was part of our extended family. So being able to sell our business as a going concern was great for the team as well as for us.

Of course you may be looking to grow your business and get backers or support from financial institutions. The principles we suggest when getting ready to sell are almost the same as when you want to get ready to expand; have a systemised profitable business that is scalable and works without you being there every day, take the right advice and market your business to potential investors.

Opening your second coffee shop will be a great challenge, as it's unlikely that you will double your sales overnight at any other time.

So it feels there is another book waiting for us to write…

TAKEAWAYS

$$Se = Th+Ro+Sy+L-Le$$

Selling =
Trading **hi**story +
Routines + **Sy**stems +
Lease - **Le**gals

The Coffee Shop Success Formula

YW + CCSL + T + WS + GP + D + Eq + EO + FC + M + Se = CSSF

Finding a clarity of **your why,** to understand the type of coffee shop you want to open, then finding a **clever coffee shop location** is only the beginning, but without getting these two elements of the equation right, your venture will have little chance of being a success. Recruiting a fantastic **team,** training, empowering and trusting them to deliver **wow service,** will give you a sound base to work on. Then selling **great products,** each with their own story, in a well-**designed** and attractive environment, will keep your guests coming back. Selecting the right **equipment** will allow you to run an **efficient operation** and keep your operational costs low. You will make a good return on your investment only if you have total **financial control**. Then using appropriate **marketing** will keep your business growing and of course you should always prepare for **selling** when the time comes.

Appendix 1 – BLOGS

We have added a selection of the most popular articles we have published. More blogs can be found on our website: www.cafesuccesshub.com/blogs

13 reasons independent coffee shops fail - 29/05/15

1. It's not a lifestyle business

The business is set up as a lifestyle business or a get rich quick scheme. A coffee shop is a real business with real guests, real overheads and a lot of potential to go wrong. It's hard work and anyone thinking that it's a great lifestyle choice will find it difficult to make money and those thinking it's a get rich quick scheme will be disappointed.

2. Arrogant owner who knows everything

Ok I know that's a bit strong, but someone who doesn't want help and carries on regardless without listening to guest or team members' feedback is heading for trouble. Having a passion is a fundamental need but when passion turns to arrogance, then the clock is ticking towards the closing sale!

3. Wrong location

Location is key - the balance between a great site in a great location with a high rent and the not so good site in a not so good location with a lower rent is a very fine balance. Sometimes if there's a lot of competition around, this is a good thing, as your guests are already coming to the area and sometimes if you are the first one in an area, then you risk been affected by any new coffee shops close by. People don't want to travel far to get their coffee, it's unlikely that you will very soon become a destination that people will travel a long way to visit, it's more likely that people will pop in as they're walking past because they are hungry or thirsty.

4. It's too small

A unit with less than about forty covers will always find it difficult to generate enough revenue to cover costs, consider that you'll need at least two people on every shift to maintain a reasonable amount of service so factor that into your costs. Having more than one floor is always a disadvantage, as people never like climbing stairs.

5. No budget or plan

Not knowing your numbers- understand what tax you will need to pay at the end of the quarter. VAT has a habit of being quite a lot more than you expect. Most things you sell will be vatable, so 20% of your sales will go directly to the taxman

Managing your cash flow and keeping on top of your bank account, the first few months the bank balance will look great, then the suppliers will need paying, next the P32's then the VAT. If you are not in control and planning for these movements in your bank account then you are in for a shock.

6. Inconsistent standards

Consistency is critical-your guests will be very regular, it becomes like a marriage where the little things niggle. Making sure that you open on time everyday, that everything you make is consistent and of good quality is very important as time goes on. As a rule of thumb people allow you to make three mistakes before they leave, the first time they put it down to experience, the second time they think you are just daft and the third time they leave you.

Your drinks must be perfect 100% of the time. If only 95% of your drinks are perfect then a daily guest will get at least one bad drink a month.

7. Poor service

Any coffee shop that does not offer great service will not get repeat business. Fantastic service comes from recruiting the best team, then training, training, training and rewarding them as much as you can. Recruit for attitude not skill and you won't go far wrong. If you pay the minimum wage, expect to lose your team quickly and have to retrain from scratch. Your guests won't like this because they get to know who works in your coffee shop and build up a friendship with them. They become more than a business and more like extended family.

8. It's got a strange name

Being too clever with the name - let people know what you do through your name so that when they're walking past they know what to expect. Match your offer to your local guests; make sure you communicate your USP through your branding. People love a story that they can tell their friends about, which is great for word-of-mouth advertising. Don't expect everyone to flock to a business called 'Eat Dirt' (real name, not made up, no longer trading).

9. No stock taking

Take stock every week- work out your profit every week. Know the cost of every item that you sell, its profit and its recipe. Control the team costs tightly, check there are no hidden costs in the rent or from the landlord and don't be tempted to spend too much money on the fit out costs.

Not having good systems, routines and processes although boring, will make sure that a lot of the things above happen when you are not in the shop.

10. No checking

Not having robust checks for cash and deliveries, will let your money trickle through your fingers. Cash and stock losses are worth twenty times the value in sales to recoup.

11. No backup

Not having a contingency fund – something will always go wrong outside of your control and you need to keep a reasonable sum of money at hand for that inevitability. Also, your café will need refitting in about three years, so you need some money to pay for that.

12. Poor equipment

One thing a coffee shop owner must invest in is a good coffee machine and grinders. A coffee shop will never make money if their coffee machine breaks down often, and I will if its not maintained. Having a seven day comprehensive service contract in place, to be able to call an engineer out as soon as the problem occurs is essential. This contract will service the grinders and coffee machine, including boiler checks. You will never have a consistent coffee if your grinders and coffee machine aren't serviced regularly.

13. Poor relationships with suppliers

Building a great relationship with your suppliers is fundamental in a successful business, pay them on time and talk to them if there any problems, if you stop paying and they stop delivering then you won't have anything to sell.

Coffee shops have a low barrier to entry- anybody can set one up. They need to be treated as proper businesses; they're not a lifestyle business that fits around you. Running one involves working long hours to get things right, it's quite physical and tiring and dictates your lifestyle.

What can coffee shops learn from pubs? – 05/05/15

The demise and re-invention of the pub that we have witnessed over the last twenty years, has a lot more to do with the future of the coffee shop than you might first think.

Pubs have suffered from relentless competition on practically all fronts in the last two decades and The Campaign for Real Ale, CAMRA, estimate that they are closing at a rate of thirty one per week. A lot of the reasons for their closing have actually been a benefit to the coffee shop industry.

Price & Availability - Up to a few years ago, the government increased the amount of tax on alcohol in every budget, which constantly increased the price of your pint, the supermarkets have benefitted massively and increased the amount of alcohol bought for home consumption. Now over twice as much alcohol is off sale compared to that bought from pubs. 'Prinks' or 'pre drinks' are what people do before going out to a pub or club because they can get their spirits raised for a fraction of the price of drinking out.

Where coffee consumption has been growing in coffee shops it has mostly been a shift from instant coffee consumption, as people become more discerning. The rise of the automatic self serve coffee machine now found everywhere from the garage to your office lobby will start doing what the supermarkets did to pubs for coffee shops.

The rise of the coffee pod machine, it's one of our favourite Christmas gifts with sales up 45% in 2013 and with the cost of pods coming down all the time since Nespresso the biggest maker of pods lost its patents, a decent coffee can be had for less than 30p per capsule at home, this will cause a shift as people no longer have to get to a coffee shop to get great coffee. These machines are so consistent that they are used in many of the world's top restaurants, so coffee shop owners should not be complacent to this threat.

Pubs have always been at a disadvantage when they have been 'tied houses' where they are only allowed to sell a certain range of beers from their brewery. The rise of the craft beer and microbreweries has transformed the fortune of many a pub. The same can be seen with the rise of the 4th wave of coffee houses. Jeffery Young of Allegra Strategies, (Young) who are the coffee industry statistician's, predicted at the London Coffee Festival in May 2015, that the science of coffee will become the 4th wave and that the chains are looking to follow into this market too, with echoes of the craft beer movement.

To survive, the pub is reinventing itself as an all day, female friendly casual dining establishment. The success of the Loungers concept is testament to this, with its fantastic growth over the last five years, it's coffee sales are a very important part of its business with the team getting coffee training on a par with any coffee shop. Wetherspoons too are using coffee as a weapon to attract guests away from coffee shops, by the offer of free refills.

In contrast the coffee shop has always been female friendly but has generally has a poor choice of food and shorter opening hours, the opportunity for the modern coffee shop is to improve the range of food it serves and open longer. There is also a fantastic opportunity for licensed coffee shops to sell craft beers and wines as well, a trend that is very evident in the London and Manchester coffee scene. The 4th wave of coffee shops will offer a variety of single origin coffees that will be made in a variety of different ways from brew bars to siphons, they will roast their own coffee on site and have the coffee knowledge to the same level a sommelier in a restaurant has about wine. They will educate their guests in the science of coffee to increase the enjoyment and discernment.

Coffee shops have always benefited from WIFI, as many pubs have been slow to realise the potential of allowing people to work effectively from their premises. This advantage is being quickly eroded with the introduction of 4G, as people are able to work from places that don't offer WIFI. The opportunity is to make it even easier and more convenient for people to work from the coffee shop, by providing electric charging facilities and a variety of seating with good lighting.

The pub companies were criticised by many for turning unprofitable managed sites to tempting opportunities for people wanting to run their own pub and then watching them loose their money and be labelled as cannon fodder. There is a trend emerging that those people who would have looked a running a pub, think they can open a coffee shop and make money. There are many coffee franchises out there if the prospective owner thinks they need the support and there are many others who just go it alone. Many of these new coffee shops open and close quickly under the radar, as they are in the wrong position, their rent is too high, the concept flawed or the franchisor does not offer the right support and is not motivated by the profitability of the franchisee.

Overall coffee shops are predicted to outnumber pubs in ten years at the current rate of growth, this seems realistic, as the UK's coffee consumption is still the lowest in per head in Europe. The opportunities for the increase in coffee sales are great but the opportunity to consume it are growing as fast or even faster than demand, so the successful coffee shop could take many lessons from the evolution of the pub. In Darwinian terms;

'It is not the most intellectual of the species that survives; it is not the strongest that survives; but the species that survives is the one that is able best to adapt and adjust to the changing environment in which it finds itself.'

Great news - food intolerance is growing! – 02/08/15

Food intolerance

It might not be a good thing for those with food intolerance, but your coffee shop can benefit from the food intolerances of your guests.

With over 35% of people saying that they have food intolerance, every café, coffee shop and restaurant needs to take this seriously.

Recent research has suggested that only 5% of adults actually have an allergy or some type of food intolerance, whereas up to 35% of people believe they actually have food intolerance.

When you add that to the growing number of vegetarians and vegans, you have a large cohort of your guests who will be very aware of your menu items.

The net impact of this is that 35% of your guests will be looking for a special diet of some type; any business that ignores this demand will lose more and more guests over time.

Group decisions are affected

In a group of guests looking to visit, the person with the special diet will be the person that chooses to visit that restaurant or café, so the impact could even be higher. In a party of four there is a very high probability that there will be a person with a special diet among them who is likely to choose where to take the party.

This is not the same issue as the healthy eating options that people say they want but never buy; people are serious about avoiding the products that they are intolerant to.

There are many early adopters of realising the importance of food intolerances. Nandos menu is mostly gluten free and La Tasca has a gluten free accredited menu.

The simplest way for us as coffee shop owners to address food intolerance is to provide different types of milk. Soya milk has been around for a long time but now there are many more varieties- rice milk, coconut milk and almond milk to name a few.

The more difficult thing for us to achieve is our food range. With many things in a coffee shop being sweet, they tend to include gluten and milk. The market is growing rapidly at the moment and more gluten-free and free from products are becoming available.

How to get the advantage

The clever café or coffee shop can use this heightened awareness of food intolerance to provide a clear advantage:

- Have the range of food intolerances that you cater for displayed clearly on your website – many people pre-plan their trips to accommodate this.
- Have a sign on your windows visible to people outside thinking of coming in, of your special diet options.
- Clearly mark on your in-store menus the options.
- Product labels also make it easy for people to decide.
- Put the range in one place so it's easier to make a choice.
- Train your team to offer suggestions – have a crib sheet available.

Of course, there are restaurants that are completely vegetarian or gluten-free for example. These cutting edge restaurants and café s will attract a cult following but for the majority of us, we will have to ensure our menu is adapted accordingly to attract the largest number of potential people with food intolerances.

Overall it's the coffee shop, café or restaurant that caters for these dietary needs well that will prosper.

First impressions matter – 25/06/15

You only get one chance to make a first impression

The university open day season is upon us and if you like us have teenage children trying to decide where to study, you will be visiting a few new places for the first time over the next few weeks. You will realise why first impressions matter so much for your business.

This is the second season of the open day tours for us, so we feel quite seasoned travellers and know what to expect. Yesterday on our visit to Plymouth University in Devon, we were absolutely blown away by the whole day and our son left very excited over the prospect of going there to study.

On the journey home, we reflected on what they did so well to have this effect on us. There are so many lessons for a coffee shop or restaurant owner to learn from it.

The welcome

Starting at the welcome, which was in the form of a massive inflatable arch at the front of the university, clearly showing you where to go.

- *How clear is your signage from 100 yards away?*

The smiles and cheery welcome, not only from the very first person we met but everyone we met throughout the day.

- *Is everyone in your business as cheery and welcoming?*

The organisation

The registration, we were greeted individually by a member of the team and asked to register using the 'Chimpadeedoo' app from MailChimp on an iPad.

- *Do you get all your guests details so you can follow up with them?*

The overall organization was great, a good guide with simple summaries of the talks and clear timings of start and finish times as well as a guide for parents.

- *How clear and easy to understand is your menu?*

Every single talk started and finished on time, with separate hand-outs for you to take away and a well-facilitated question time included.

- *Do you always open on time and deal with your guests concerns or requests respectfully?*

Every talk had an associated display of work from current students with testimonials from lots of happy students.

- *How well do you use your current guests to market your business, do you use testimonials and reviews to your advantage?*

There were tea and coffee available at every session and free food available on campus. This kept us engaged for longer, as normally our day is spent looking for places to get a drink and some food that is away from the main campus.

- *What do you do to make sure your guests stay longer and spend more?*

Finally, it seemed that the town was geared up for the influx in guests as well, with busy restaurants and bars.

- *How much notice of local events do you take when planning your week trade for team cover and food prep?*

Follow up

The next day we received a parent follow-up survey as well to find out what we thought about the day.

- *How many times do you ask for feedback from your guests?*

Plymouth University did everything so well and out of the 10 university open days we have been to, it was by far the best. Our experience has only made our son more likely to apply there.

With the cost of a university course being nearly £50k and with only one chance to get your business, they have maximised their chances of being at the top of the application form.

In the same way, it's the lifetime spend of your guest you are trying to capture on their first visit.

You only get one chance to make a first impression - that's why 'first impressions matter.'

When free coffee causes chaos, a lesson in understanding for Waitrose – 16/05/15

Waitrose, the upmarket British grocer has been the centre of much media attention over the last few weeks, all over their policy of giving away free coffee to their customers. It seems there are lots of people who don't like the idea and are getting hot under the collar. Social media is reacting, customers are complaining, politicians are getting involved, local business owners are upset.

This all comes about because in 2011 Waitrose developed a plan to get more footfall into its shops, rather than discount its prices which can be up to 50% more expensive than its rivals, it started to give away a free coffee and a free newspaper to all their My Waitrose card holders, their free to join loyalty programme.

All you needed to do was to come into the store and show your card to get a free coffee, if you bought a newspaper with other items the cost of the newspaper was deducted from your bill as well. A win - win for everyone you might think. The company was very happy with the increase in footfall it was getting and the scheme seemed to be working, as the net effect was people were spending more money when they visited the store to get a free coffee. Waitrose became the second biggest provider (we can't say seller) of coffee in the UK seemingly overnight, just behind McDonalds! The queues for coffee were the longest of any in the store.

Then the customers started complaining that it was attracting the 'wrong type of customer' to their oasis of poshness and causing health and safety issues with the potential spilling of hot coffee! 'Please don't turn Waitrose into a soup kitchen' a customer posted on the Waitrose Facebook page.

The local business's complained it was unfair competition, with one coffee shop owner taking Waitrose to the Office of Fair Trading. They decided to take no action.

MP's have waded in, Andy Sawford the labour MP for Corby wrote to all MP's with Waitrose in their constituency saying that it was having a detrimental effect to small businesses.

It now costs Waitrose £150,000 per week to run the scheme, which gives away a million cups of coffee a week, that is probably quite an underestimate of the cost. The capital cost of a few hundred coffee machines that are not generating any revenue, the repair and maintenance and team costs need to be included here as well.

The problem is its business is still falling, as in March 2015 Aldi overtook it in terms of market share. Fundamentally Waitrose pricing is at the top end of the range and with growth of the discounter, it's never been easier to save money on your grocery shopping and their price difference is up to 50% more than the discounters. So although they have been getting more customer traffic for their free coffee, their overall customer spend must be declining.

They are now trying to tighten up the criteria for the free coffee, which is causing even more furore on social media and in the press. This is a natural reaction as when you give something away and then try to start charging, people's value perception of that product is very low. Coffee has a big value gap in as much as it is a low-cost product with lots of added value. That added value is normally provided in the environment of the coffee shop that serves it. When it's from a machine then that added value is eroded.

Their loyal customer base, the same one that complained about attracting the wrong sort of customers, now feels entitled to a free coffee!

The moral of the story, know your customers needs and desires and the type of new customers that you want to attract. Set up a limited time offer and review the results carefully, you can then extend and delight or stop and not disappoint your customers.

Here is a link to a buzzfeed post that sums up the situation really well.

http://www.buzzfeed.com/scottybryan/i-just-want-my-free-coffee#.paV2W6okp

Lets have a picnic in your coffee shop! – 11/08/15

We have spotted a growing trend recently where guests smuggle their own food or food they have bought elsewhere to eat in the comfort of our Coffee Shop, effectively having a picnic. They seem to believe that because they have bought a drink it's ok to tuck into a bag of chip's or a sandwich they have brought in with them.

Where have these incredibly bad manners come from? It's inconceivable that they would feel free to take their own food into a restaurant, even MacDonald's, unpack it and start eating, so why is it acceptable to do the same in a coffee shop?

When we ask them politely to not eat other people food in our establishment pretty much everyone is embarrassed and know what they are doing is bad form. They have normally found an area that is quiet and private where they think they won't get caught surreptitiously stuffing their face with illicit food.

We have recently had to tell people eating kebabs in the comfort of our chairs that not only was it not allowed but also the smell of the fried food was very upsetting for the rest of the guests.

Why is it suddenly OK?

Ok we can understand baby food or a kids favourite snack here and if our food was outrageously expensive or not of the highest quality, then we possibly could understand why people may be tempted to do it, but it's not. It's all made fresh every day and is reasonably priced to complement our finely crafted coffees and teas. We've even put up signs to the effect as well, telling people they are only allowed to eat food bought on the premises.

What are the best upselling techniques in coffee shops? — 11/07/15

Why is upselling a dirty word?

Most of us have a poor perception of anyone involved in sales, however, we forget that without selling we have no business.

Our teams have the same mind-set and when you talk to them about upselling at the till, they often have a mental barrier to trying to get guests to spend more than they intended to when they walked through the door.

Upselling is vital to the health of your business and can add a significant amount of turnover. A muffin upsell to a guest buying a coffee can be 100%.

Opportunity

So if you can upsell to one in four guests you could increase your sales by 25%.

We were lucky enough to meet Steve Clarke of UK Sales Mentor recently, he talked about his time mystery shopping opticians and the lack of up selling done by the optometrists because their professional reluctance to sales. This lack of up selling almost cost him his sight as only one out of the six opticians he visited offered him the most thorough eye test because it was more expensive. You need to get his book by the way from www.eurekasales.co.uk (Clarke).

So an extra muffin or a danish pastry as an upsell is not quite in the same league as saving someone's sight but it can make someone's day to enjoy that little treat they had been craving for, or they could discover a whole new flavour that they had never experienced before.

We can use mystery shoppers, training, and supervision and still not get past the idea in our teams minds that it is rude to sell and they don't like to be pushy, so are naturally reluctant to upsell for us.

Mindset

If we can change the mindset of our teams so that they see an up-selling opportunity as an opportunity to make someone's day, then we will see a significant improvement in our bottom line and well as the number of happy guests.

What upselling techniques do you use in your coffee shop? What do you do in your business that ensures everyone upsells automatically for you? Please let us know if you have cracked it or if it still frustrates you.

Will your coffee shop survive a crisis? – 17/06/15

Would your business survive a crisis?

The recent tragic events at Alton Towers theme park, when two roller coasters collided caused serious injury and lots of publicity, has got me thinking how my small business would cope with a crisis of its own.

Ok, we sell coffee and cakes, so it's unlikely that something of the same magnitude could happen in our business, or is it? There are a number of similarities between theme parks and coffee shops, we serve thousands of people per week, we generally employ young people and liquids are involved although ours are hot where Splash Mountain is cold!

You only need to open your newspaper to find a restaurant that has had a food scare or poor health inspector visit, this will have a dire effect on trade to the point that many of the businesses will never get over the bad publicity and they will close.

Following the principles below will help:

- Have a solid documented legally compliant operating procedure
- Train every team member to understand and follow the guidelines and record their training
- Record the checks that are made to ensure that the processes are followed
- Review, and record your review of the whole system
- Have good insurance, including business interruption and key man policies

Small issues become big problems

A key thing to remember is that how you deal with any crisis, however small is important. A stray hair in a sandwich could become a major issue is if not dealt with well by the team straight away. We are constantly reminded of the fact that a complaint will spread much faster than a compliment and in the age of instant communication to thousands or millions of people via social media. Your stray hair could become a food contamination issue that tarnishes your reputation for years and gets you a visit from the local environmental health department. TripAdvisor reviews will be affected; Google always seems to pick up on the bad reviews as well.

The cost of all this can be quite small in comparison to the impact on your business, being a member of the Federation of Small Businesses in the UK (FSB) will provide you with legal advice and your local Environmental Health Department will be able to provide you with documentation and advice. They much prefer helping you do a good job rather than finding faults at an inspection.

There are so many things where the responsibility is down to the business now rather than a third party authority, risk assessments for equipment & COSHH, electrical safety testing are things that could be easily overlooked or ignored to save money but when an issues occur, it will be the business owner that will be personally liable and if the correct procedures have not been completed, then the insurance company will not pay out.

Even the best are vulnerable

We know of a restaurant that was run with the highest standards, the chef was very uncooperative with an EHO visit, which resulted in a Zero Star rating, this was reported in the local paper and is still on the internet. This resulted in a dramatic loss of trade for a 6-month period. They are now recovering, it illustrates that even the best operators can be affected.

Can you sleep at night?

It's essential that your operating policies and procedures are legally compliant, robust and easy to follow by team members. Spending time and money by taking expert advice at the beginning of your business journey is very worthwhile and will allow you to sleep at night. If your business does not have these things in place then now may be the time to review them.

Are your toilets driving you mad? – 07/07/15

Are your toilets being abused?

With the decline in local public toilet facilities provided by the councils, your local coffee shop is the favourite destination of many people needing to answer the call of nature and a lot of them think it ok to not buy anything from you.

The problem is that every time someone uses your toilet it costs you money and is a part of your overhead that is often not covered by a matching purchase, as a growing number of people believe it ok to use your facilities even though they don't buy anything from you.

Have you calculated the cost of each flush to you, water in, water out, maintenance repairs, team cost to clean, cleaning chemicals, toilet roll, air freshener, hand drier electricity, opportunity cost of the space used. 30p a flush is not an unrealistic estimate.

Of course, to add insult to injury, you are already paying for the provision of a public toilet in your business rates as well.

How can you manage the need of your guests, whilst reducing abuse? We need to provide a toilet facility for our guests and locks and codes will make their lives harder, but conversely abuse by non-guests will also prevent them using the facilities and often lead to less clean toilets as well.

There are a number of different points of view, with some owners happy to allow everyone to use their toilet in the hope that a % of people will purchase something, others keep it locked and only available via a code or a key from the till, thus causing some inconvenience to their real guests. Signage doesn't seem to work and charging is not really appropriate, so what can we do?

Works Cited

Young, J. (n.d.). From http://www.allegrastrategies.com/

BSA. (n.d.). *Beverage Standards Association*. From www.beveragestandardsassociation.co.uk

Clarke, S. (n.d.). *UK Sales Mentor*. From www.eurekasales.co.uk

Egolf, D. B. *Forming Storming Norming Performing: Successful Communication in Groups And Teams*.

FSB. (n.d.). *Federation of Small Businesses*. From http://www.fsb.org.uk/

Gerber, M. *The E Myth Revisited*.

Gilmartin, H., & Richardson, J. *Wake Up and Smell the Profit: 52 Guaranteed Ways to Make More Money in Your Coffee Business*.

Gilmartin, H., & Richardson, J. *Setting Up and Managing Your Own Coffee Bar: How to open a coffee bar that actually lasts and makes money . . . (Coffee Boys Step By Step Guide)*.

Kolenda, N. (n.d.). From http://www.nickkolenda.com/psychological-pricing-strategies/

Mayer, D. *Setting the Table: The Transforming Power of Hospitality in Business [SETTING THE TABLE: THE TRANSFORMING POWER OF HOSPITALITY IN BUSINESS]*.

Oxford Mail. (2013, 4 22). From http://www.oxfordmail.co.uk/news/10370017.Pair_s_web_coffee_fa d_a__perc__for_homeless/

Oxford Mail. (2014, 5 29). From http://www.oxfordmail.co.uk/news/top_news/11241715.Extra_cups_ of_coffee_add_up_to_a_big_boost_for_homeless/

Oxford Mail. (2014, 10 1). From http://www.oxfordmail.co.uk/news/11505484.Coffee_day_stirs_up_i nterest/

SCAE. (n.d.). From http://www.scae.com/

Slalom. (n.d.). From https://www.slalom.com/thinking/visual- analytics-101-the-art-and-science-of-color

Made in the USA
Middletown, DE
13 September 2018